Reading and Note Taking Study Guide

ECONOMICS

SAVVAS
LEARNING COMPANY

Contents
Economics
Reading and Note Taking Study Guide

Topic 10
Trade, Development, and Globalization

How to use the *Reading and Note Taking Study Guide*

The **Reading and Note Taking Study Guide** will help you better understand the content of Savvas *Economics*. This section will also develop your reading, vocabulary, and note taking skills. Each study guide consists of three components. The first component focuses on developing graphic organizers that will help you take notes as you read.

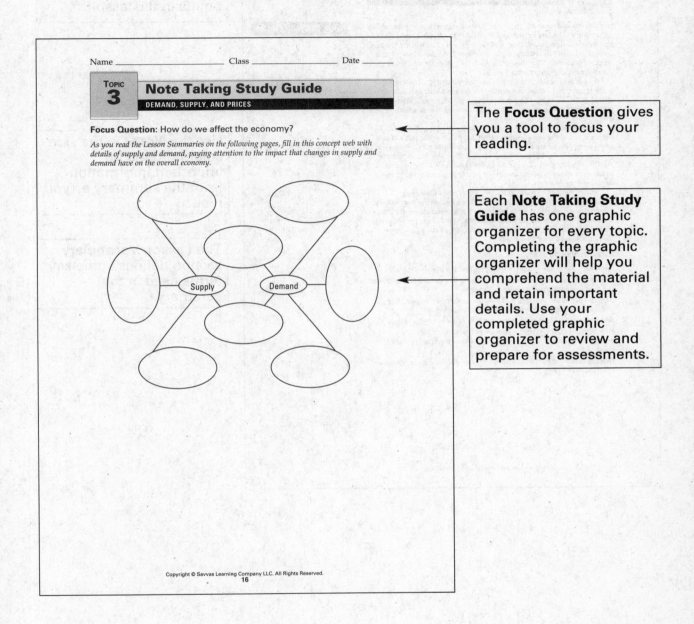

Name _____ Class _____ Date _____

TOPIC 3

Note Taking Study Guide

DEMAND, SUPPLY, AND PRICES

Focus Question: How do we affect the economy?

As you read the Lesson Summaries on the following pages, fill in this concept web with details of supply and demand, paying attention to the impact that changes in supply and demand have on the overall economy.

Supply   Demand

The **Focus Question** gives you a tool to focus your reading.

Each **Note Taking Study Guide** has one graphic organizer for every topic. Completing the graphic organizer will help you comprehend the material and retain important details. Use your completed graphic organizer to review and prepare for assessments.

The second component highlights the central themes, issues, and concepts of each lesson.

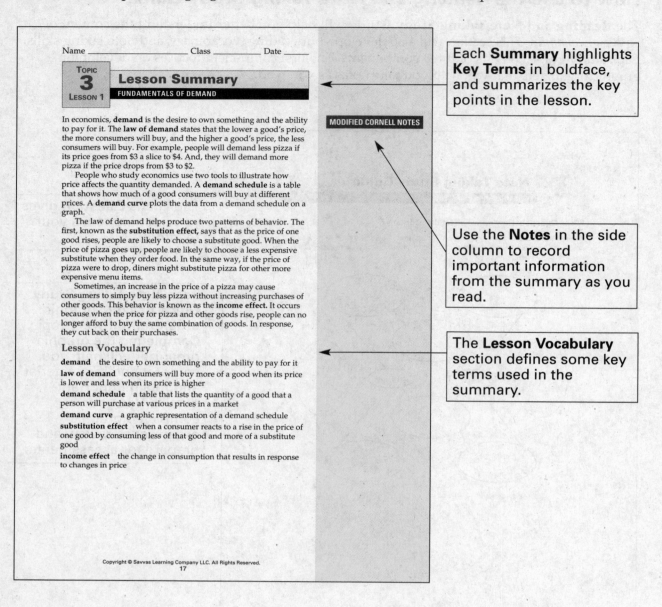

Name _____ Class _____ Date _____

Lesson Summary
FUNDAMENTALS OF DEMAND

In economics, **demand** is the desire to own something and the ability to pay for it. The **law of demand** states that the lower a good's price, the more consumers will buy, and the higher a good's price, the less consumers will buy. For example, people will demand less pizza if its price goes from $3 a slice to $4. And, they will demand more pizza if the price drops from $3 to $2.

People who study economics use two tools to illustrate how price affects the quantity demanded. A **demand schedule** is a table that shows how much of a good consumers will buy at different prices. A **demand curve** plots the data from a demand schedule on a graph.

The law of demand helps produce two patterns of behavior. The first, known as the **substitution effect,** says that as the price of one good rises, people are likely to choose a substitute good. When the price of pizza goes up, people are likely to choose a less expensive substitute when they order food. In the same way, if the price of pizza were to drop, diners might substitute pizza for other more expensive menu items.

Sometimes, an increase in the price of a pizza may cause consumers to simply buy less pizza without increasing purchases of other goods. This behavior is known as the **income effect.** It occurs because when the price for pizza and other goods rise, people can no longer afford to buy the same combination of goods. In response, they cut back on their purchases.

Lesson Vocabulary

demand   the desire to own something and the ability to pay for it

law of demand   consumers will buy more of a good when its price is lower and less when its price is higher

demand schedule   a table that lists the quantity of a good that a person will purchase at various prices in a market

demand curve   a graphic representation of a demand schedule

substitution effect   when a consumer reacts to a rise in the price of one good by consuming less of that good and more of a substitute good

income effect   the change in consumption that results in response to changes in price

MODIFIED CORNELL NOTES

Each **Summary** highlights **Key Terms** in boldface, and summarizes the key points in the lesson.

Use the **Notes** in the side column to record important information from the summary as you read.

The **Lesson Vocabulary** section defines some key terms used in the summary.

The third component consists of review questions that assess your understanding of the lesson.

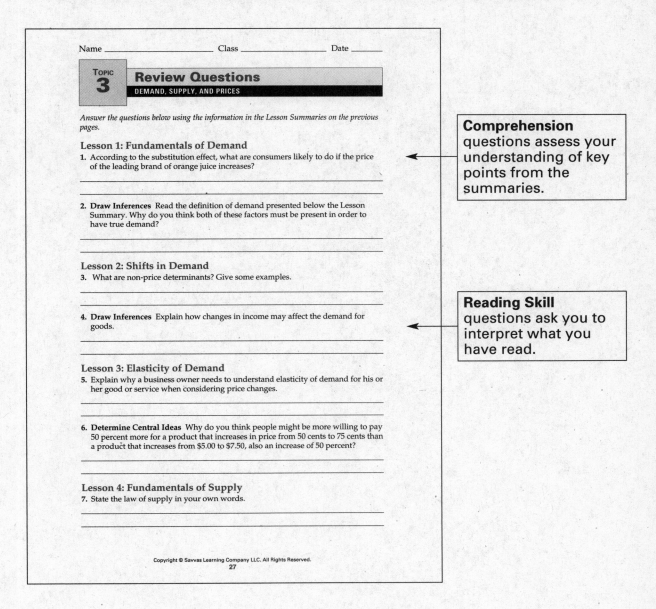

Name _____ Class _____ Date _____

Answer the questions below using the information in the Lesson Summaries on the previous pages.

Lesson 1: Fundamentals of Demand

1. According to the substitution effect, what are consumers likely to do if the price of the leading brand of orange juice increases?

_____

_____

2. **Draw Inferences** Read the definition of demand presented below the Lesson Summary. Why do you think both of these factors must be present in order to have true demand?

_____

_____

Lesson 2: Shifts in Demand

3. What are non-price determinants? Give some examples.

_____

_____

4. **Draw Inferences** Explain how changes in income may affect the demand for goods.

_____

_____

Lesson 3: Elasticity of Demand

5. Explain why a business owner needs to understand elasticity of demand for his or her good or service when considering price changes.

_____

_____

6. **Determine Central Ideas** Why do you think people might be more willing to pay 50 percent more for a product that increases in price from 50 cents to 75 cents than a product that increases from $5.00 to $7.50, also an increase of 50 percent?

_____

_____

Lesson 4: Fundamentals of Supply

7. State the law of supply in your own words.

_____

_____

27

Comprehension questions assess your understanding of key points from the summaries.

Reading Skill questions ask you to interpret what you have read.

vii

TOPIC 1

Note Taking Study Guide

FUNDAMENTALS OF ECONOMICS

Focus Question: How does economics affect everyone?

As you read the Lesson Summaries on the following pages, complete the outline below to organize and summarize the content of this section.

I. Scarcity

   A. Needs and wants

     1.

     2.

   B. What is scarcity?

     1.

     2.

II. Opportunity costs and trade-offs

   A.

     1.

     2.

   B.

     1.

     2.

III. Production possibilities curves

   A.

     1.

     2.

   B.

     1.

     2.

Name _____ Class _____ Date _____

Lesson Summary

SCARCITY

MODIFIED CORNELL NOTES

People always have to make decisions about how to meet their needs and wants. A need is something people must have to survive, like air, food, and shelter. A want is something that people would like to have but is not necessary for survival. Economics is the study of how people choose from limited resources to meet their needs and wants.

People have to make such choices because of scarcity, the limited amounts of **resources** to meet unlimited desires. Goods are objects, like cars and clothes. Services are actions that people do for others, such as teaching. A shortage occurs when a good or service is unavailable. Shortages occur when people have trouble supplying goods and services at current prices. Shortages may occur because of situations like war or **drought**. They may end quickly or last a long time.

Economists call the resources used to make goods and services factors of production. There are three types: land, labor, and capital. Land includes natural resources like coal, water, and forests. Labor is work for which people receive pay. Capital is a human-made resource used to produce other goods and services. Objects made by people, like buildings and tools, are called physical capital. Human capital refers to the knowledge and skills people gain from study and experience. Entrepreneurs are people who put together land, labor, and capital to create new businesses.

Lesson Vocabulary

resources something that a country or business can use to increase its wealth

drought a long period of time during which there is very little or no rain

Name _____ Class _____ Date _____

MODIFIED CORNELL NOTES

When making decisions, people face **trade-offs**, or alternatives we give up when we choose one course of action over another. Individuals, businesses, and governments all face trade-offs. A person who chooses to spend more time at work has less time to spend at home. A business that uses all of its factories to build chairs cannot build tables at the same time. A country that decides to produce more military goods has fewer resources to use for consumer goods. Economists use the term **guns or butter** to describe this trade-off.

A person who chooses one alternative gives up other alternatives. The most desirable alternative given up is called the **opportunity cost**. For example, suppose you have to choose between sleeping late or getting up early to study for a test. The opportunity cost of extra study time is less sleep. The opportunity cost of more sleep is less study time.

Decisions also involve **thinking at the margin**. This means deciding about adding or subtracting one unit of a resource, such as one hour of sleep. In the example above, the decision was between sleeping late or studying. But you could also choose to sleep an hour late, then wake up to study. To make a decision at the margin, you would compare the opportunity cost and benefit of each extra hour of studying. The benefit of adding one more unit of anything, such as one more hour of studying, is called the **marginal benefit**. The cost of adding one more unit of anything is called the **marginal cost.** The process of making decisions based on costs and benefits is called a **cost/benefit analysis**.

Lesson Vocabulary

trade-off   the act of giving up one benefit in order to gain another, greater benefit

guns or butter   a phrase expressing the idea that a country that decides to produce more military goods ("guns") has fewer resources to produce consumer goods ("butter") and vice versa

opportunity cost   the most desirable alternative given up as the result of a decision

thinking at the margin   the process of deciding whether to do or use one additional unit of some resource

marginal benefit   the extra benefit of adding one unit

marginal cost   the extra cost of adding one unit

cost/benefit analysis   a decision-making process in which you compare what you will sacrifice and gain by a specific action

TOPIC 1 LESSON 3	**Lesson Summary**
	PRODUCTION POSSIBILITIES CURVES

MODIFIED CORNELL NOTES

Economists use graphs that are called **production possibilities curves** to show alternative ways of using a country's resources. For example, an economist might want to examine the production of shoes and watermelons. A production possibilities curve can show how the number of shoes produced is affected by the number of watermelons grown. As the number of watermelons produced is increased, the number of shoes produced will decrease. This happens because land is scarce, and more land for watermelon farms means less land for shoe factories. Similarly, as more shoes are produced, fewer resources are available to grow watermelons.

Efficiency means an economy is using resources in such a way as to maximize the production of goods and services. In the above example, efficiency would mean that the most watermelons and shoes possible are being produced. The line on the curve that shows the maximum possible production is called the **production possibilities frontier**. If factory workers and farmers lost their jobs, fewer shoes and watermelons would be produced. In this case, the economy would suffer from **underutilization**, or using fewer resources than it is capable of using. A country's resources are always changing.

In the future, resources may increase, causing the economy to grow. If more labor becomes available, there will be more workers to produce more goods. Improvements in technology, or know-how, will also help the economy grow. This growth can be shown by a shift to the right on the production possibilities frontier.

Lesson Vocabulary

production possibilities curve a graph that shows alternative ways to use a country's productive resources

efficiency the use of resources in such a way as to maximize the output of goods and services

production possibilities frontier a line on a production possibilities curve that shows the maximum possible output an economy can produce

underutilization the use of fewer resources than an economy is capable of using

Name _____ Class _____ Date _____

Answer the questions below using the information in the Lesson Summaries on the previous pages.

Lesson 1: Scarcity

1. What are two examples of goods and two examples of services?

_____

_____

2. Draw Inferences What is an example of the kinds of choices that a business would have to make because of scarcity?

_____

_____

Lesson 2: Opportunity Cost and Trade-Offs

3. Use your own words to describe the trade-off known as "guns or butter."

_____

_____

4. Identify Cause and Effect Why does every decision involve a trade-off?

_____

_____

Lesson 3: Production Possibilities Curves

5. If a country chose to produce twice as many wooden chairs as before, how would that affect its production of wooden tables?

_____

_____

6. Apply Concepts Many countries produce a single good upon which much of their economy depends. That good might be coffee or wool or oil. How might a production possibilities curve help economists in such a country determine how to diversify their economy?

_____

_____

Name _____ Class _____ Date _____

Note Taking Study Guide
FREE ENTERPRISE AND OTHER ECONOMIC SYSTEMS

Focus Question: Who benefits from the free market economy?

As you read this section, take notes in the following chart to summarize the content. Be sure to identify key questions or details that explain the benefits of free market economic systems.

Economic Questions	Economic Systems	Economic Growth
•	•	•
•	•	•
•	•	•

TOPIC 2 LESSON 1

Lesson Summary
THE THREE KEY ECONOMIC QUESTIONS

Because economic resources are limited, a country must answer three key economic questions. These are: 1) What goods and services should be produced? 2) How should these goods and services be produced? 3) Who consumes these goods and services? All countries must answer these questions in deciding how to use their scarce economic resources.

In answering these questions, societies must consider their economic goals. Some goals, such as economic freedom or economic equity, are considered more important in some countries than in others. Other goals, like economic efficiency, are shared by most countries. Another important goal is growth and **innovation**, which is the process of bringing new methods, products, or ideas into use. A nation's economy must grow in order to improve its **standard of living**, or level of prosperity.

Societies may develop different additional economic goals, such as protecting the environment and full employment. Societies can also have goals that conflict with one another. For example, providing a **safety net** that helps protect people from economic turmoil may come at the cost of growth.

Several types of economic systems have developed as societies attempt to answer the three key economic questions according to their goals. An **economic system** is the method a society uses to produce and distribute goods and services. The oldest and simplest economic system is the **traditional economy**, which relies on custom to make most economic decisions. People grow up doing what their parents did, and there is little innovation or change.

Lesson Vocabulary

innovation the process of bringing new methods, products, or ideas into use

standard of living level of economic prosperity

safety net a set of government programs that protect people who face unfavorable economic conditions

economic system the structure of methods and principles that a society uses to produce and distribute goods and services

traditional economy an economic system that relies on habit, custom, or ritual to decide the three key economic questions

TOPIC 2 LESSON 2

Lesson Summary
FREE MARKETS

MODIFIED CORNELL NOTES

None of us can produce everything we need and want. Markets exist so that people can exchange the things they have for the things they want. A **market** is an arrangement that allows buyers and sellers to exchange goods and services.

A **free market economy** is one of the main economic systems. It is a system in which answers to the basic economic questions are produced by the decisions of buyers and sellers freely exchanging goods and services in the marketplace.

Markets function because of self-interest and competition. **Self-interest** means buyers and sellers are focused on their own personal gain. Self-interest motivates consumers to buy goods and services they want at the lowest prices possible. **Competition** is the struggle between producers for the dollars of consumers. Competition keeps prices low and quality high as firms try to attract consumers. Together, self-interest and competition work to regulate the marketplace.

The factor market and the product market are the two main parts of the free market. In the **factor market**, firms purchase land, labor, and capital—the factors of production—from households. Firms rent land, hire workers, and borrow money from investors. In the **product market**, households purchase goods and services produced by firms.

The free market helps an economy meet many economic goals. It encourages efficiency, economic freedom, and innovation and growth. However, two other economic goals—security and equity—can be more challenging in a pure market system. Many societies have modified the free market system to better meet their goals.

Lesson Vocabulary

market   any arrangement that allows buyers and sellers to exchange things

free market economy   an economic system in which decisions on the three key economic questions are based on voluntary exchange in markets

self-interest   an individual's own personal gain

competition   the struggle among producers for the dollars of consumers

factor market   the arena of exchange in which firms purchase the factors of production from households

product market   the arena of exchange in which households purchase goods and services from firms

Name _____ Class _____ Date _____

TOPIC
2
LESSON 3

Lesson Summary
CENTRALLY PLANNED ECONOMIES

In a **centrally planned economy**, the central government, rather than individual producers and consumers in markets, answers the key economic questions about production and consumption. The government owns the land and the capital. It controls where people will work and how much they will be paid. It decides what is produced and at what price things will be sold. This type of economy is also called a **command economy**.

The terms **socialism** and **communism** are associated with centrally controlled economies. Socialists attach great value to the goal of economic equity. They believe that economic equality is possible only if the public controls the economy. Socialist countries may be democracies. Communists share many of the goals of socialists, but believe that these goals can only achieved through violent revolution.

In a communist society, government is **authoritarian**. It requires obedience from its people and denies them personal freedom. The former Soviet Union was an example of a communist nation where most economic and political power was controlled by the central government. Under the Soviet system, all workers were guaranteed employment and income. Factories and farms had to meet production goals set by the government. China is another communist nation with an authoritarian government. But China has in recent times allowed some economic freedom.

Centrally planned economies try to promote faster economic growth and more equal distribution of goods and services. However, these systems almost always fall short of their goals. Without the incentive of self-interest, producers have no reason to produce more or better products. Consumers find it difficult to meet their needs or wants, having to accept poorly made merchandise. In addition, individual freedoms are limited.

Lesson Vocabulary

centrally planned economy   an economic system in which the government makes all decisions on the three key economic questions

command economy   another name for a centrally planned economy

socialism   a range of economic and political systems based on the belief that wealth should be distributed evenly throughout a society

communism   a political system in which the government owns and controls all resources and means of production and makes all economic decisions

authoritarian   describes a form of government that limits individual freedoms and requires strict obedience from its citizens

	TOPIC 2 LESSON 4	**Lesson Summary**
		MIXED ECONOMIES

No economic system can achieve every economic goal. Even the free market system has drawbacks. In fact, even the strongest supporters of free markets recognize that there is a role for government in the economy. For example, people know that free markets would have difficulty providing for national defense or for highways. Government generally provides these services. Government also plays a role in protecting people's right to own **private property**, which is property owned by a person and not a government.

No country has an economy that is purely free market or purely controlled by the government. All are **mixed economies**, combining free markets with some government involvement. The amount of government involvement varies from country to country. At one extreme, the North Korean economy is almost completely controlled by the government. China has a centrally planned economy but undergoing **economic transition**, in which it is moving toward a market system. Compared to most countries, the United States has free markets with limited government involvement. Singapore and Hong Kong are examples of economies with even less government involvement.

Lesson Vocabulary

private property   property that is owned by individuals or companies, not by the government or the people as a whole

mixed economy   economic system that has some market-based elements and some level of government involvement

economic transition   a period of change in which a nation moves from one economic system to another

Name _____ Class _____ Date _____

MODIFIED CORNELL NOTES

There is a tradition of free enterprise in the United States—a tradition that encourages people to try out their business ideas and compete in the public market. The American economy provides **open opportunity**, which means anyone can enter and compete in the marketplace. Everyone is free to make their own agreements and their own decisions.

In the free enterprise economy, consumers, acting on their own, decide to buy products. Their individual choices signal the producers what to produce and how much to make. Consumers can also join together to form **interest groups** to try to get the market or government to meet their wants and needs. Entrepreneurs step in to meet these needs and wants. The **profit motive**, or the desire to earn a profit, helps guide them to meet consumer demand. As a result, the market produces a variety of products at reasonable prices.

Government laws, such as those protecting the right to private property and enforcing contracts, help Americans benefit from free enterprise. The Constitution also specifies how government can tax, and it prohibits government from interfering in business contracts. Finally, federal and state agencies regulate industries whose goods and services affect the well-being of the public.

Lesson Vocabulary

open opportunity   the principle that anyone can compete in the marketplace

interest group   a private organization that tries to persuade public officials to act in ways that benefit its members

profit motive   the incentive that drives individuals and business owners to improve their material well-being

TOPIC 2 LESSON 6

Lesson Summary
SUPPORTING ECONOMIC GROWTH

To keep the huge American economy on course, government economists follow macroeconomic trends. **Macroeconomics** is the study of the behavior and decision making of entire economies. By contrast, **microeconomics** is the study of economic behavior of individuals, families, and businesses. Macroeconomic progress is measured by calculating the nation's **gross domestic product (GDP)**. This is the total value of all final goods and services produced in a year. Measuring the change in GDP from one year to the next is one way of measuring growth or decline in an economy.

Free enterprise systems are subject to sudden swings in **business cycles**, the repeating pattern of macroeconomic growth followed by slowing or decline. To stabilize the economy and prevent wide swings, the government has three main goals: high employment, steady economic growth, and stable prices. Government policymakers use different policies and tools in their attempts to achieve these goals.

One way Americans maintain their high standard of living is by constantly improving technology. Technology is the process used to produce a good or service. Progress in technology helps the economy to be more efficient and productive. For example, Thomas Edison's invention of the light bulb in 1879 made possible a longer work day. To advance technological progress, government policies encourage innovation. Federal agencies fund research and development projects at universities and private companies. The government also provides **patents**, which help inventors profit from new ideas. **Copyrights** help authors of creative works profit from them. These protections encourage inventors and creative people to create innovation and new ideas.

Lesson Vocabulary

macroeconomics   the study of economic behavior and decision making in a nation's whole economy

microeconomics   the study of economic behavior and decision making in small units, such as households and firms

gross domestic product (GDP)   the total value of all final goods and services produced in a country in a given year

business cycle   a period of macroeconomic expansion, or growth, followed by a period of contraction, or decline

patent   a government license that gives the inventor of a new product the exclusive right to produce and sell it

copyright   a government license that grants an author exclusive rights to publish and sell creative works

Lesson Summary
PUBLIC GOODS AND EXTERNALITIES

MODIFIED CORNELL NOTES

People depend on the government to provide public goods. A **public good** is a shared good or service for which it would be inefficient or impractical to make consumers pay individually. Examples of public goods are roads, dams, and national defense. If the government did not provide these things, individuals or companies would have to do so themselves. But for an individual, the cost of building a highway outweighs the benefits. So, without government assistance, the highway would likely not be built. Another characteristic of a public good is that it is difficult to exclude those who do not pay for it. For example, once a road is built, it is difficult to keep drivers from using it. Situations like these, in which the free market does not efficiently use resources to solve a problem, are known as **market failures**.

Public goods are paid for by the **public sector**. The public sector is the part of the economy which involves government transactions. The **private sector** involves transactions of individuals and businesses.

Externalities can affect the public and private sector. An **externality** is an economic side effect of a good or service. Education, for example, is a service that benefits students. But there is a side effect: Society as a whole benefits from an educated population. The government encourages the creation of positive externalities. The government also works to limit negative externalities, such as automobile pollution. Not everyone agrees that government is better than the market at dealing with negative externalities.

Government is involved in protecting people from the effects of poverty. **Welfare** is a general term for government aid to the poor. Some critics worry that by providing aid to the poor, government makes people dependent on welfare.

Lesson Vocabulary

public good a shared good or service for which it would be inefficient or impractical to make consumers pay individually and to exclude those who did not pay

market failure a situation in which the free market, operating on its own, does not distribute resources efficiently

public sector the part of the economy that involves the transactions of the government

private sector the part of the economy that involves the transactions of individuals and businesses

externality an economic side effect of a good or service that generates benefits or costs to someone other than the person deciding how much to produce or consume

welfare government aid to the poor

TOPIC 2 — Review Questions
FREE ENTERPRISE AND OTHER ECONOMIC SYSTEMS

Answer the questions below using the information in the Lesson Summaries on the previous pages.

Lesson 1: The Three Key Economic Questions

1. Use context clues to come up with a definition of the phrase *economic equity*.

_____
_____

2. **Distinguish Among Fact, Opinion, and Reasoned Judgment** *People in societies with traditional economies tend to rely on established technologies, have access to limited goods, and lack modern conveniences, but they love what they do for work.* What part of the preceding statement is an opinion? Explain your answer.

_____
_____

Lesson 2: Free Markets

3. In your own words, describe what a free market economy is.

_____
_____

4. **Determine Meaning** One of the advantages of a free market is consumer sovereignty. Why do consumers hold such power in a free market system? Give a specific example to support your answer.

_____
_____

Lesson 3: Centrally Planned Economies

5. What method do centrally planned economies generally rely upon to control labor?

_____
_____

6. **Generate Explanations** Why do you think all communist governments have been authoritarian in nature?

_____
_____

Lesson 4: Mixed Economies

7. Why are mixed economies so prevalent?

_____
_____

8. **Draw Conclusions** What do you think may be some of the inherent reasons why nations today do not have pure free market economies?

_____
_____

Lesson 5: Benefits of Free Enterprise

9. How does the tradition of free enterprise impact the availability of consumer products?

_____

_____

10. Draw Inferences What kind of person makes a good entrepreneur? List at least two personality traits of a successful entrepreneur.

_____

_____

Lesson 6: Supporting Economic Growth

11. Using the terms *macroeconomic* and *microeconomic*, explain the economic relationship between a nation and the firms and households that are in that nation.

_____

_____

12. Draw Conclusions If you pay attention to the news, you probably hear a lot about national economic data such as unemployment or gross domestic product (GDP). If you have a steady job, why should you care how the rest of the country is doing?

_____

_____

Lesson 7: Public Goods and Externalities

13. Provide an example of a public good that is not in the lesson summary.

_____

_____

14. Cite Evidence to explain why infrastructure is a public good.

_____

_____

TOPIC 3	**Note Taking Study Guide**
	DEMAND, SUPPLY, AND PRICES

Focus Question: How do we affect the economy?

As you read the Lesson Summaries on the following pages, fill in this concept web with details of supply and demand, paying attention to the impact that changes in supply and demand have on the overall economy.

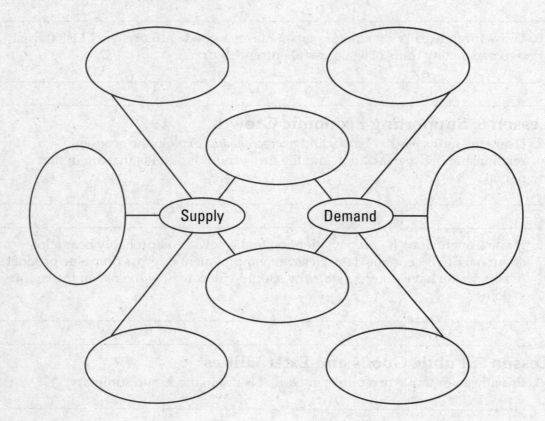

TOPIC 3 LESSON 1

Lesson Summary
FUNDAMENTALS OF DEMAND

In economics, **demand** is the desire to own something and the ability to pay for it. The **law of demand** states that the lower a good's price, the more consumers will buy, and the higher a good's price, the less consumers will buy. For example, people will demand less pizza if its price goes from $3 a slice to $4. And, they will demand more pizza if the price drops from $3 to $2.

People who study economics use two tools to illustrate how price affects the quantity demanded. A **demand schedule** is a table that shows how much of a good consumers will buy at different prices. A **demand curve** plots the data from a demand schedule on a graph.

The law of demand helps produce two patterns of behavior. The first, known as the **substitution effect,** says that as the price of one good rises, people are likely to choose a substitute good. When the price of pizza goes up, people are likely to choose a less expensive substitute when they order food. In the same way, if the price of pizza were to drop, diners might substitute pizza for other more expensive menu items.

Sometimes, an increase in the price of a pizza may cause consumers to simply buy less pizza without increasing purchases of other goods. This behavior is known as the **income effect.** It occurs because when the price for pizza and other goods rise, people can no longer afford to buy the same combination of goods. In response, they cut back on their purchases.

Lesson Vocabulary

demand   the desire to own something and the ability to pay for it

law of demand   consumers will buy more of a good when its price is lower and less when its price is higher

demand schedule   a table that lists the quantity of a good that a person will purchase at various prices in a market

demand curve   a graphic representation of a demand schedule

substitution effect   when a consumer reacts to a rise in the price of one good by consuming less of that good and more of a substitute good

income effect   the change in consumption that results in response to changes in price

Lesson Summary
SHIFTS IN DEMAND

MODIFIED CORNELL NOTES

The law of demand relates to how price affects demand when all other factors stay the same. In fact, many other factors besides price can affect demand. These factors are called **non-price determinants** of demand. For example, if the weather became very hot, people may desire less hot pizza. Consumers buy less pizza at all price levels. This change in demand at all price levels is called a demand shift, or a change in demand. On the demand curve, a demand shift moves the entire curve to the right or left.

Many factors can shift the demand curve. Changes in income is one example. Higher income causes people to buy more of most goods at every price level. Similarly, a decrease in income causes demand for most goods to fall.

Changes in **demographics,** or the makeup of the population, will affect demand. For example, the aging of the population is likely to increase the demand for medical care. Advertising and fashion trends can also have a big effect on consumer demand.

A change in demand for one good can shift demand for other goods. **Complements** are two goods that are bought and used together. People who buy skis are likely to buy ski boots, so a change in one will affect the other. **Substitutes** are goods used in place of one another. When people buy more snowboards they will buy fewer skis.

Lesson Vocabulary

non-price determinant   factors other than price that can affect demand for a particular good or service

demographics   the statistical characteristics of populations and population segments, especially when used to identify consumer markets

complements   two goods that are bought and used together

substitutes   goods that are used in place of one another

TOPIC 3 LESSON 3

Lesson Summary
ELASTICITY OF DEMAND

Economists use the term **elasticity of demand** to describe the way people respond to price changes. If you keep buying despite a price increase, your demand is **inelastic.** If you buy a lot less after a small price increase your demand is **elastic.** Demand tends to be inelastic for goods that have few substitutes, like medicines, or for goods that are considered essential, like milk. Demand is often elastic for luxury items.

Economists have a mathematical formula they use to measure elasticity of demand. The formula calculates the ratio of change in demand to change in price. If there is less than a one-to-one ratio of change in demand to change in price, demand is inelastic. If there is a greater than one-to-one ratio, demand is elastic.

Elasticity is an important tool for business owners. It helps them to determine how a change in prices will affect their business's **total revenue,** or the amount of money the company receives by selling its goods. If a business faces elastic demand for its good or service, then raising prices will result in a sharp drop in demand. This may decrease total revenue. However, when a good has an inelastic demand, a business might be able to increase prices and sell the same quantity of its good or service. In that case, the business would enjoy an increase in total revenue.

Lesson Vocabulary

elasticity of demand   a measure of the way quantity supplied reacts to a change in price

inelastic   describes demand that is not very sensitive to price changes

elastic   describes demand that is very sensitive to a change in price

total revenue   the total amount of money a company receives by selling goods or services

Name _____ Class _____ Date _____

MODIFIED CORNELL NOTES

Supply is the amount of a good or service that is available to consumers. As the price of a good rises, firms will increase the **quantity supplied,** or the amount of the good or service they offer to the market. New firms will have an incentive to enter the market. The tendency of suppliers to offer more of a good at a higher price is called the **law of supply.** This law states that the higher the price, the larger the quantity supplied. If the price of a good falls, less of a good will be supplied.

Economists record data about how price affects supply on a table called a **supply schedule.** They also create **supply curves,** which are graphs that show how changes in price affect quantity supplied. For example, a supply curve could show the quantity of pizza supplied at different prices. A supply curve always rises from left to right. That is because higher prices encourage producers to supply more of that good or service to the market.

Elasticity of supply is a concept that describes how suppliers react to price changes. Industries that cannot easily alter quantity supplied in response to price changes have inelastic supply. Orange growers, for example, cannot quickly grow more oranges when prices for oranges rise. They need to purchase more land and plant more trees in order to increase output. A barbershop, however, may have a more elastic supply, meaning it can alter its supply quickly in response to price changes. If the price of a haircut rises, barbershops and salons can hire new workers or increase hours quickly.

Lesson Vocabulary

supply   the amount of a good or service that is available

quantity supplied   the amount of a good or service that a producer is willing and able to supply at a specific price

law of supply   producers offer more of a good or service as its price increases and less as its price falls

supply schedule   a chart that lists how much of a good or service a supplier will offer at various prices

supply curve   a graph of the quantity supplied of a good or service at various prices

elasticity of supply   a measure of the way quantity supplied reacts to a change in price

TOPIC **3** LESSON 5	## Lesson Summary
	COSTS OF PRODUCTION

Economists divide a producer's costs into fixed costs and variable costs. A **fixed cost** is a cost that does not change, no matter how much the business produces. Examples of fixed costs include rent and the purchase of machinery. A **variable cost** is a cost that rises or falls depending on the quantity of good produced. These include the costs of raw materials and some labor. Fixed and variable costs together add up to produce the **total cost.**

Businesses can increase output by hiring more workers or purchasing more machinery. The change in output from adding one more worker is called the **marginal product of labor.** Often, adding one new worker will result in **increasing marginal returns,** meaning the output of goods per worker goes up. This happens because adding more workers may allow people to specialize and fully use tools or machinery. But at some point, adding new workers may no longer increase output per worker, and the business will experience **diminishing marginal returns.** For example, workers may need to wait to use a tool or machine. As more workers are added and they begin to get in each other's way, there can eventually be **negative marginal returns,** in which each new worker actually lowers total output.

(Continues on the next page.)

Lesson Vocabulary

fixed cost   a cost that does not change no matter how much of a good or service is produced

variable cost   a cost that rises or falls depending on the quantity produced

total cost   the sum of fixed costs and variable costs

marginal product of labor   the change in output that results from hiring one additional unit of labor

increasing marginal return   the level of production in which the marginal product of labor increases as the number of workers increases

diminishing marginal return   the level of production in which the marginal product of labor decreases as the number of workers increases

negative marginal return   when the addition of a unit of labor actually reduces total output

TOPIC 3 LESSON 5

Lesson Summary
COSTS OF PRODUCTION (continued)

MODIFIED CORNELL NOTES

Marginal cost is the cost of producing one more unit of a good. **Marginal revenue** is the revenue gained from producing one more unit of a good, and it is equal to the market price of the unit on the market. When marginal cost is less than marginal revenue, a producer has an incentive to increase output, since it will earn a profit on the next unit produced. When marginal cost is more than marginal revenue, a producer has an incentive to decrease output, since it will lose money on the next unit produced. That is why profits are maximized when marginal cost equals marginal revenue.

Lesson Vocabulary

marginal cost   the cost of producing one more unit of a good or service

marginal revenue   the additional income from selling one more unit of a good or service; sometimes equal to price

Lesson Summary
CHANGES IN SUPPLY

MODIFIED CORNELL NOTES

The law of supply explains how supply changes in response to price changes when all other factors are constant. But all other factors are not always constant. Many non-price determinants can affect supply and cause it to change at all price levels. For example, any change in the cost of inputs, such as raw materials, machinery, or labor, will affect supply at all price levels. A cost increase for inputs causes a drop in supply at all prices because the good has become more expensive to produce.

A change of supply at all price levels is called a shift in supply. That is because a change in supply causes the entire supply curve to shift. On a graph, an increase in supply causes the supply curve to shift to the right. A decrease in supply causes the curve to shift to the left.

The government has the power to cause supply shifts. A **subsidy** is a government payment to support a business or market. Since the subsidy lowers producers' costs, it is likely to cause an increase in supply. The government can also reduce the supply of some goods by placing an excise tax on them. An **excise tax** is a tax on the production or sale of a good, making it more expensive to produce. **Regulation,** or steps the government takes to control production, may also affect supply.

Producers' expectations are another influence on supply. If sellers expect the price of a good to rise in the future, they will store goods now and sell more in the future. But if the price of the good is expected to drop, sellers will put more goods on the market immediately.

Lesson Vocabulary

subsidy a government payment that supports a business or market

excise tax a tax on the production or sale of a good

regulation government intervention in a market that affects the production of a good

MODIFIED CORNELL NOTES

TOPIC **3** LESSON 7	**Lesson Summary**
	EQUILIBRIUM AND PRICE CONTROLS

In a market, **equilibrium** is the point at which quantity supplied and quantity demanded are equal. It is the price at which buyers are willing to buy the same quantity of a good or service that the sellers are willing to sell. On a graph, equilibrium is the point where the supply curve and the demand curve meet.

A market is said to be in **disequilibrium** when the quantity supplied does not equal the quantity demanded. When disequilibrium occurs, market forces push the market back toward equilibrium.

When quantity demanded is more than quantity supplied, there is excess demand, or a **shortage**. Shortage occurs when prices somehow fall lower than the equilibrium price, which encourages buyers and discourage sellers. When a shortage occurs, sellers are likely to raise their prices so they can earn more profits. In time, the price increase will lower demand, and the market will again reach an equilibrium point, where supply and demand are the same.

When quantity supplied is more than quantity demanded, there is excess supply, or a **surplus**. Prices will fall because sellers need to sell their supply.

Sometimes governments attempt to control prices in a market. Governments may set a **price ceiling**, a maximum price that can be charged for a good or service. For example, some cities have price ceilings on rental apartments. If the price ceiling is lower than the equilibrium price, a shortage will result. Property owners will offer fewer apartments than people want to rent.

Governments may also set a **price floor**, a lowest price that can be paid. An example is the **minimum wage**, the lowest hourly rate a business can pay workers. When a minimum wage is higher than the equilibrium rate, a surplus of labor may occur.

Lesson Vocabulary

equilibrium   the point at which the demand for a product or service is equal to the supply of that product or service

disequilibrium   any price or quantity not at equilibrium; when quantity supplied is not equal to quantity demanded in a market

shortage   a situation in which consumers want more of a good or service than producers are willing to make available at a particular price

surplus   when quantity supplied is more than quantity demanded

price ceiling   a maximum price that can legally be charged for a good or service

price floor   a minimum price for a good or service

minimum wage   a minimum price that an employer can pay a worker for an hour of labor

Name _____ Class _____ Date _____

TOPIC 3 LESSON 8

Lesson Summary
CHANGES IN MARKET EQUILIBRIUM

MODIFIED CORNELL NOTES

Free markets tend to seek equilibrium. If a price for a good or service leads to excess supply or demand, market forces push the price up or down until supply and demand are again equal. Sometimes, however, changes in market conditions lead to the shift of an entire demand curve or supply curve. This means that the quantity demanded or supplied changes at all price levels. Such changes also create disequilibrium. When this occurs, market forces seek to establish a new equilibrium point, a price where the new supply and demand meet.

Technology, for example, can make a good cheaper to produce. The earliest digital cameras cost many hundreds of dollars. Then technology improved, lowering the cost of making the cameras. The price of cameras also dropped. The supply curve shifted to the right as producers were willing to offer greater quantities of cameras at all prices. However, quantity supplied was now greater than quantity demanded, leading to a surplus. Producers reacted to the surplus by lowering prices, and eventually price and quantity reached a new equilibrium.

A shift in demand can be caused by a fad, such as the surge in popularity of a new toy. The demand curve shifts, reflecting the fact that buyers are willing to buy more toys at every price. At the old equilibrium price, demand is now greater than supply, creating a shortage. Producers respond by raising prices and increasing supply, until once again the quantity supplied equals the quantity demanded and a new equilibrium is established.

Lesson Vocabulary

free market A market in which individuals determine what gets made, how it is made, and how much people can consume of goods and services produced

Name _____ Class _____ Date _____

MODIFIED CORNELL NOTES

In a free market, prices serve several important functions. Prices are like signals that send information to buyers and sellers. For producers, a high price is a signal to increase supply. A low price is a signal to reduce the supply or leave the market. For buyers, a low price is a signal and an incentive to buy. A high price is a signal to think before buying.

Another key feature of prices is that they are flexible. Prices can usually change more quickly than production levels. Consider the example of a **supply shock,** which is a sudden shortage of a good. If a natural disaster destroys a crop, for example, supply cannot be quickly restored. But prices can change quickly, helping reduce excess demand.

There are options to the price system. **Rationing** is a system for allocating goods and services using tools other than price. When rationing is in place, people are told what and how much of a good they can consume. Centrally planned economies use rationing, not price, to distribute goods and services. Rationing is expensive to administer. There is generally little variety of goods available, as producers have little incentive to respond to the demands of consumers. Rationing also leads to the appearance of **black markets,** which are illegal markets for the exchange of goods outside the rationing system.

Prices do not always work efficiently in markets in which there is not much competition, or in which buyers and sellers do not have enough information. Another inefficiency in markets involve negative externalities, such as air and water pollution. These are side effects of production that producers do not have to pay and that are not reflected in the prices consumers pay.

Lesson Vocabulary

supply shock   a sudden shortage of a good

rationing   a system of allocating scarce goods and services using criteria other than price

black market   a market in which goods are sold illegally, without regard for government controls on price or quantity

TOPIC 3 — Review Questions
DEMAND, SUPPLY, AND PRICES

Answer the questions below using the information in the Lesson Summaries on the previous pages.

Lesson 1: Fundamentals of Demand

1. According to the substitution effect, what are consumers likely to do if the price of the leading brand of orange juice increases?

_____

_____

2. **Draw Inferences** Read the definition of demand presented below the Lesson Summary. Why do you think both of these factors must be present in order to have true demand?

_____

_____

Lesson 2: Shifts in Demand

3. What are non-price determinants? Give some examples.

_____

_____

4. **Draw Inferences** Explain how changes in income may affect the demand for goods.

_____

_____

Lesson 3: Elasticity of Demand

5. Explain why a business owner needs to understand elasticity of demand for his or her good or service when considering price changes.

_____

_____

6. **Determine Central Ideas** Why do you think people might be more willing to pay 50 percent more for a product that increases in price from 50 cents to 75 cents than a product that increases from $5.00 to $7.50, also an increase of 50 percent?

_____

_____

Lesson 4: Fundamentals of Supply

7. State the law of supply in your own words.

_____

_____

8. **Identify Cause and Effect** Would a lawn care business have elastic or inelastic supply in the short term? Explain your answer.

_____

_____

Lesson 5: Costs of Production

9. What are the four types of costs that a business must consider in making business decisions?

_____

_____

10. **Identify Cause and Effect** What are the causes and effects of increasing marginal returns?

_____

_____

Lesson 6: Changes in Supply

11. Explain how and why rising and falling input costs affect supply.

_____

_____

12. **Draw Inferences** If government regulation increases price and thus decreases supply, why does the government regulate any goods and services?

_____

_____

Lesson 7: Equilibrium and Price Controls

13. *Equilibrium* means "balance." What is out of balance when a market is in a state of disequilibrium?

_____

_____

14. **Identify Cause and Effect** Consider the market conditions that exist in the event of a shortage. Explain what role price has on both buyers and sellers in this situation.

_____

_____

Name _____ Class _____ Date _____

Lesson 8: Changes in Market Equilibrium

15. What are the two factors that can push a market into disequilibrium?

_____

_____

16. Draw Conclusions You see a poster in a store window that says, "Pre-Winter Sandal Blowout." Why do you think a store might offer a big discount on sandals in the fall?

_____

_____

Lesson 9: Prices at Work

17. How do you know, as a consumer shopping for a product, whether goods are in short supply or are readily available?

_____

_____

18. Summarize Explain why the price system leads to greater choice for consumers than is available in centrally planned systems.

_____

_____

Name _____ Class _____ Date _____

Focus Question: How does competition affect markets?

As you read the Lesson Summaries on the following pages, take notes in the chart below summarizing the role competition plays in the types of markets listed.

Pure Competition	Monopolies
<ul><li></li><li></li><li></li></ul>	<ul><li></li><li></li><li></li></ul>
Monopolistic Competition and Oligopoly	**Government Regulation and Competition**
<ul><li></li><li></li></ul>	<ul><li></li><li></li></ul>

Name _____ Class _____ Date _____

MODIFIED CORNELL NOTES

The simplest market structure to study is one known as **pure competition**. In such a market, every firm produces the same product for about the same price. Because each firm produces a small part of the total supply, no one firm can control the price. In order to have pure competition a market must meet four conditions. It must have many buyers and sellers participating. Sellers must offer identical products. Products that are the same no matter who makes them are called **commodities**. Buyers and sellers must be well informed about the products. Sellers must be able to enter and leave the market easily.

Only a few industries come close to meeting these conditions. Two examples are the market for farm products and the stocks traded on a stock exchange.

Factors that make it difficult for new firms to enter a market are called **barriers to entry**. Common barriers to entry include start-up costs and technology. **Start-up costs** are the expenses an owner has to pay before opening a new business. For example, before starting a new sandwich shop, you would have to rent a store, buy cooking equipment, and print menus. Other businesses require technical ability. Carpenters, pharmacists, or electricians need training before they can have the skills they need.

Purely competitive markets are efficient. The intense competition in these markets keeps both prices and production costs low. A firm that raised its prices higher than other firms, or experienced higher production costs, would not be able to compete.

Lesson Vocabulary

pure competition   a market structure in which a large number of firms all produce the same product and no single seller controls supply or prices; also called perfect competition

commodity   a product, such as petroleum or milk, that is considered the same no matter who produces or sells it

barriers to entry   any factor that makes it difficult for a new firm to enter a market

start-up costs   the expenses a new business must pay before it can begin to produce and sell goods

Name _____ Class _____ Date _____

A **monopoly** is a market dominated by a single seller. Instead of many buyers and sellers, as is the case with pure competition, a monopoly has one seller and any number of buyers. Barriers to entry make monopolies possible. Monopolies can take advantage of their monopoly power and charge high prices. For this reason, the United States has outlawed monopolistic practices in most industries.

The government allows monopolies in certain industries. A **natural monopoly** is a market that runs most efficiently when one large firm provides all the output. In the local telephone industry, a monopoly developed because it was inefficient for more than one company to build an expensive wire network. In such cases, the government may give one company the right to dominate a geographic area. In return, that company will agree to let the government control its prices.

The government can also grant monopoly power by issuing patents or licenses. A **patent** gives a company exclusive rights to sell a new good or service for a specific time period. A **license** is a government-issued right to operate a business. Radio licenses give a station the right to broadcast at a certain frequency.

Unlike firms in purely competitive markets, monopolists have control over prices. However, the law of demand means that when the monopolist raises the price, it will sell fewer goods. So the monopolist sets a price that maximizes its profit. This usually means fewer goods, at a higher price, than would be sold in a more competitive market.

Monopolists also try to maximize profits by using **price discrimination**. This means that the monopolist charges different groups of customers different prices for the same product. Price discrimination can only work if the good is difficult to resell and if it easy to divide customers into groups that will pay different prices.

Lesson Vocabulary

monopoly   a market in which a single seller dominates

natural monopoly   a market that runs most efficiently when one large firm provides all of the output

patent   a license that gives the inventor of a new product the exclusive right to sell it for a specific period of time

license   a government-issued right to operate a business

price discrimination   the division of consumers into groups based on how much they will pay for a good

TOPIC 4 LESSON 3

Lesson Summary

MONOPOLISTIC COMPETITION AND OLIGOPOLY

Pure competition and monopoly are the two extremes in the range of market structures. Most markets fall into two other categories: **monopolistic competition** and oligopoly. Monopolistic competition is a market in which many companies sell products that are similar but not identical. For example, jeans can differ in brand, style, and color. Ice cream differs in taste and flavors. These markets are called monopolistic competition because each firm has a kind of monopoly over its own particular product. Monopolistic competition exists in industries where there are low barriers to entry.

Firms that are monopolistically competitive have slight control over their prices, because they offer products that are slightly different from any other company's. They also use **non-price competition**, or competition through ways other than lower prices, to compete. They may offer new colors, textures, or tastes in their products. They may also try to find the best location for their services.

Oligopoly is a market dominated by a few large firms. It can form when significant barriers to entry exist. Examples of oligopolies in the United States include air travel, breakfast cereals, and household appliances. Oligopolistic firms sometimes use illegal practices to set prices or to reduce competition. They may engage in **collusion**, which is an agreement among firms to set prices or production levels. One type of collusion is **price fixing**, which means agreeing to charge the same or very similar prices. Price fixing is illegal in the United States and can lead to heavy penalties.

Lesson Vocabulary

monopolistic competition   a market structure in which many companies sell products that are similar but not identical

non-price competition   a way to attract customers through style, service, or location, rather than a lower price

oligopoly   a market structure in which a few large firms dominate a market

collusion   an illegal agreement among firms to divide the market, set prices, or limit production

price fixing   an agreement among firms to charge one price for the same good

Name _____ Class _____ Date _____

MODIFIED CORNELL NOTES

Monopoly and oligopoly can sometimes have negative effects on consumers and our whole economy. Markets dominated by only a few large firms tend to have higher prices and lower output than markets with many sellers. A firm with monopoly power can use **predatory pricing**. This is the practice of setting the market price below cost to drive competitors out of business. Another way firms try to reduce competition is by buying out their competitors.

Since the late 1800s, the United States has had **antitrust laws** to prevent companies from reducing competition. It is the job of the Federal Trade Commission and the Department of Justice's Antitrust Division to enforce these laws. The government also tries to prevent mergers that might reduce competition and lead to higher prices. A **merger** is when two or more companies join to form a single firm.

In the 1970s and 1980s, Congress passed laws leading to the deregulation of some industries. **Deregulation** is the lifting or reducing of government controls over a market. Markets experiencing deregulation included the airline, electricity, banking, railroad, natural gas, and television broadcasting industries. When it is successful, deregulation increases competition and leads to lower prices for consumers. However, it may often cause hardship for employees of companies driven out of business by increased competition.

Antitrust laws strengthen government control over a market. Deregulation loosens government control. Yet both policies have the same purpose: to promote competition.

Lesson Vocabulary

predatory pricing   selling a product below cost for a short period of time to drive competitors out of the market

antitrust laws   laws that encourage competition in the marketplace

merger   when two or more companies join to form a single firm

deregulation   the removal of government controls over a market

Name _____ Class _____ Date _____

Answer the questions below using the information in the Lesson Summaries on the previous pages.

Lesson 1: Pure Competition

1. What makes a product a commodity?

_____

_____

2. **Identify Cause and Effect** Why would high start-up costs serve as a barrier to competition?

_____

_____

Lesson 2: Monopolies

3. Give three examples of price discrimination.

_____

_____

4. **Draw Conclusions** Why must a monopoly supply a good or service that has no close substitute?

_____

_____

Lesson 3: Monopolistic Competition and Oligopoly

5. How do monopolistically competitive firms compete with each other and differentiate their products?

_____

_____

6. **Support Ideas with Examples** Why is location a factor in non-price competition? Give an example in your answer.

_____

_____

Lesson 4: Government Regulation and Competition

7. Who might be the "prey" in a predatory pricing scheme?

_____

_____

8. **Identify Cause and Effect** When the government deregulates an industry, what does it expect will happen?

_____

_____

TOPIC 5

Note Taking Study Guide

BUSINESS AND LABOR

Focus Question: How can businesses and labor best achieve their goals?

As you read the Lesson Summaries, complete the following outline to summarize the content of this section.

I. **Business structures**

    A. Sole proprietorships

        1. _____

        2. _____

    B. Partnerships

        1. _____

        2. _____

    C. Corporations

        1. _____

        2. _____

II. **Labor force and wages**

    A. _____

        1. _____

        2. _____

    B. _____

        1. _____

        2. _____

    C. _____

        1. _____

        2. _____

TOPIC 5 LESSON 1

Lesson Summary
SOLE PROPRIETORSHIPS

MODIFIED CORNELL NOTES

One of the first decisions an entrepreneur must make is what kind of business organization he or she will have. In other words, what structure will the ownership of the entrepreneur's company have? The most common form of business organization in the United States is the **sole proprietorship,** which is a business owned and run by one person. More than 70 percent of all businesses in the United States are sole proprietorships. However, since most sole proprietorships are small, they account for only about 4 percent of all United States sales. Your local bakery, barber shop, and bicycle repair shop are likely to be sole proprietorships.

The greatest advantage of a sole proprietorship is that the owner gets to keep all profits after paying income taxes. Another advantage is that sole proprietorships are easy to start. They can usually be opened with a small amount of paperwork and legal expense. A sole proprietor also has complete control of his or her business, and can respond quickly to changes in the marketplace.

The most important disadvantage of sole proprietorships is unlimited personal liability. **Liability** is the legal obligation to pay debts. If a sole proprietorship fails, the owner may have to sell personal property to cover debts. Another disadvantage is that it may be hard for a sole proprietor to find capital to expand his or her business. It may also be hard to find good employees because many sole proprietors cannot afford to provide employees with **fringe benefits** such as paid vacations, retirement pay, and health insurance.

Lesson Vocabulary

sole proprietorship   a business owned and managed by a single individual

liability   the legal obligation to pay debts

fringe benefits   payments to employees other than wages or salary

Lesson Summary
PARTNERSHIPS AND FRANCHISES

A **partnership** is a business organization owned by two or more persons. The partners must agree on how profits and responsibilities are divided. The most common type of partnership is a **general partnership**, in which all partners share equally in both responsibility and liability. In a **limited partnership**, only one partner is required to be a general partner. That partner has control over the business and unlimited personal liability for the firm's actions. Other, limited partners contribute only money and can lose only their initial investment. In a **limited liability partnership (LLP)**, all partners are limited partners and are shielded from personal liability in certain situations.

Although partnerships have the advantage of being easy and inexpensive to start up, most experts advise partners to work with an attorney to develop **articles of partnership**. This legal document describes each partner's economic rights and responsibilities. Another advantage of a partnership is that the responsibility for the business may be shared. In a successful partnership, each partner brings different strengths and skills to the business. In addition, each partner's **assets**, or money and other valuables, improve the partnership's ability to borrow funds for operations or expansion.

Partnerships also have disadvantages. Each general partner is responsible for the acts of the other partners. Unless the partnership is an LLP, at least one partner has unlimited liability. Like sole proprietors, general partners can lose their own personal property in paying the firm's debts. Another potential problem is conflict among the partners. They need to come to agreement about business goals and philosophies.

(Continues on the next page.)

Lesson Vocabulary

partnership   business organization owned by two or more persons who agree on a specific division of responsibilities and profits

general partnership   a type of partnership in which all partners share equally in both responsibility and liability

limited partnership   a type of partnership in which only one partner is required to be a general partner, while other partners have limited responsibilities?

limited liability partnership   a type of partnership in which all partners are limited partners

articles of partnership   a partnership agreement that spells out each partner's rights and responsibilities

assets   the money and other valuables belonging to an individual or business

TOPIC 5 LESSON 2

Lesson Summary
PARTNERSHIPS AND FRANCHISES (continued)

A **business franchise** is a semi-independent business that pays fees to a parent company. In return, the franchise owner gets the exclusive right to sell a certain product or service in a given area. The parent company, or franchiser, develops the products and business system and helps the local franchise owners produce and sell their products. For a small business owner, a franchise has the advantage of having a built-in reputation. Other advantages may include training, support, and financing provided by the parent company. However, the franchise owner must give up some freedom. He or she must follow strict operating guidelines and offer only approved products. Another disadvantage is that the franchise owner pays a share of earnings called **royalties** to the parent company.

Lesson Vocabulary

business franchise   a semi-independent business that pays fees to a parent company in return for the exclusive right to sell a certain product or service in a given area

royalties   the share of earnings that a franchise owner pays to the parent company

Name _____ Class _____ Date _____

TOPIC 5 LESSON 3

Lesson Summary
CORPORATIONS

Most large businesses in the United States are corporations. A **corporation** is a legal entity owned by individual stockholders. Each stockholder has limited liability for the firm's debts, and can lose only as much as he or she has invested. Stockholders own **stocks**, which represent their share of ownership in the corporation. Like a person, a corporation pays taxes, can enter into contracts, and can bring lawsuits in court. All corporations have the same basic structure. Stockholders elect a board of directors. The board makes the important decisions for the corporation. It also appoints corporate officers who run the corporation.

An important advantage of the corporate structure is that it limits liability for stockholders. Stockholders can only lose the amount of money they have invested. Another advantage that corporations have is the opportunity for growth. Corporations can raise money by selling stocks on the stock market. They can also borrow money. A **bond** is a certificate that a corporation issues that includes a promise to repay borrowed money with interest at fixed intervals. In addition, the owners of a corporation, the stockholders, do not have to run the company. Instead, the corporation can hire experts to manage business operations. Lastly, because stocks are transferrable, a corporation can do business indefinitely.

Some disadvantages of corporations include difficulty of start up, potential loss of control by a company's founders, and more legal requirements and government regulations than other types of business organizations.

(Continues on the next page.)

Lesson Vocabulary

corporation   a legal entity, or being, owned by individual stockholders, each of whom has limited liability for the firm's debts

stock   a certificate of ownership in a corporation

bond   a formal contract issued by a corporation or other entity that includes a promise to repay borrowed money with interest at fixed intervals

Lesson Summary
CORPORATIONS (continued)

MODIFIED CORNELL NOTES

As a corporation grows, it may decide to merge, or combine, with another company or companies. **Horizontal mergers** join two or more firms in the same market. For example, two automakers may decide to form a larger company. Vertical mergers join two or more firms involved in different stages of making the same good or service. A **vertical merger** can allow a company to operate more efficiently. For example, an automaker may merge with the company that supplies it with tires. **Conglomerates** combine companies that produce completely unrelated goods or services. **Multinational corporations (MNCs)** are corporations that operate in more than one country at a time.

Lesson Vocabulary

horizontal merger   the combination of two or more firms competing in the same market with the same good or service

vertical merger   the merger of two or more firms involved in different stages of producing the same good or service

conglomerate   a business combination merging more than three businesses that produce unrelated products or services

multinational corporation   a large corporation that produces and sells its goods and services in more than one country

TOPIC 5 LESSON 4

Lesson Summary
NONPROFIT ORGANIZATIONS

Some businesses are not set up to earn profits. Instead, their goal may be to work for the good of members or to benefit society in some way. Two such organizations are cooperatives and nonprofit organizations.

A **cooperative** is a business organization owned and operated by a group of people for their shared benefit. **Consumer cooperatives** sell merchandise to their members at reduced prices. Cooperatives that provide a service rather than goods are called service cooperatives. Some **service cooperatives** offer discounted insurance, banking services, health care, legal help, or baby-sitting services. **Producer cooperatives** are agricultural marketing cooperatives that help members sell their products.

Nonprofit organizations function like businesses but do not operate for profit. They are usually in the business of serving society in some way. Some examples include museums, public schools, and YMCAs. The government exempts nonprofit organizations from income taxes so long as they meet certain requirements. This tax break serves as an incentive to encourage nonprofits to provide services that for-profit businesses may not provide. Some nonprofits are nongovernmental organizations (NGOs) that raise money and use it to fund and carry out programs. **Professional organizations** serve the needs of people in different occupations. **Business associations** promote business interests in a city, state, or other geographical area. **Trade associations** promote the interests of particular industries. **Labor unions** are organized groups of workers that strive to improve working conditions, hours, wages, and benefits for their members.

Lesson Vocabulary

cooperative   a business organization owned and operated by a group of individuals for their shared benefit

consumer cooperative   a retail outlet owned and operated by consumers that sells merchandise to members at reduced prices

service cooperative   a type of cooperative that provides a service rather than a good

producer cooperative   an agricultural marketing cooperative that helps members sell their products

nonprofit organization   an institution that functions much like a business but does not operate for the purpose of making a profit

professional organization   a nonprofit organization that works to improve the image, working conditions, and skill levels of people in particular occupations

business association   a nonprofit group organized to promote the collective business interests of an area or a group of similar businesses

trade association   a nonprofit organization that promotes the interests of a particular industry

labor unions   organized groups of workers that strive to improve working conditions, hours, wages, and benefits for their members

Lesson Summary
THE LABOR FORCE

Economists define the **labor force** as nonmilitary workers over 16 who are employed or unemployed. To be counted as unemployed, a person must either have work lined up in the near future or be actively looking for work. People in the military and people who are not looking for work, such as students, full-time parents, and retirees, are not considered part of the labor force. The Bureau of Labor Statistics (BLS) surveys households to collect data about the labor force. It reports the data it collects, including the monthly unemployment rate, on the Internet.

The job market changes over time. One trend in the U.S. economy is the shift from manufacturing to services. This change has resulted in a loss of manufacturing jobs. **Outsourcing**, a practice in which an employer contracts with another company to do a specific job that might otherwise have been done by the employer's own workers, has also led to job losses in the United States. So has **offshoring**, which is the movement of some of a company's operations or resources of production to other countries.

The labor force itself is also changing. More and more, workers need to have education beyond high school to obtain jobs with higher wages. Data show that earning potential increases with education level. Another important trend is the increasing number of women in the workplace. Changing social roles have encouraged many women to gain education and employment skills.

(Continues on the next page.)

Lesson Vocabulary

labor force   all nonmilitary people who are employed or unemployed

outsourcing   the practice of contracting with another company to do a specific job that would otherwise be done by a company's own workers

offshoring   the movement of some of a company's operations, or resources of production, to another country

MODIFIED CORNELL NOTES

Yet another trend is the rise of **contingent employment**, or temporary and part-time work. Companies use contingent employment to gain flexibility and to save money. It is easier to discharge temporary workers than permanent employees, so firms can quickly adjust the number of workers to increase or decrease output.

Foreign-born workers also have an effect on the labor force. Some of these workers are guests workers, who are allowed to live and work in the United States temporarily. A company can hire guest workers if they can show that they cannot fill a labor need with native-born workers.

Economists also study wages and benefits of workers. In recent years, wages of U.S. workers have decreased. Greater competition from foreign companies, deregulation of industries, and increased use of temporary workers have contributed to this decrease. Meanwhile, benefits such as pensions and health insurance are becoming more expensive for employers. Hiring contingent employees who don't receive these benefits is one way for employers to save money. Offshoring and outsourcing are other ways.

Lesson Vocabulary

contingent employment   temporary and part-time jobs that are given to workers instead of full-time or permanent jobs

Name _____ Class _____ Date _____

In a free market economy, the price of labor—the wage rate—is determined in part by the demand and supply of workers. Demand for labor comes from companies and government agencies that hire workers to produce goods and services. This labor demand is called a **derived demand** because it depends on the demand for a good or a service. If more people want to buy a product, for example, more workers are needed to produce the product. Competition for workers will push up the wages of these workers. As wages for a particular type of work increase, more people will want to do that work. Eventually, when the supply of workers meets the demand for workers, an **equilibrium wage** is set.

Jobs can be classified into four skill levels. **Unskilled labor** requires no specialized skills or training. **Semi-skilled labor** requires minimal specialized skills and education. **Skilled labor** requires specialized skills and training. **Professional labor** requires advanced skills and education. Demand for workers with higher skill levels is greater, and the supply of workers lower. As a result, the equilibrium wage is higher. Differences in working conditions also affect wage levels. Fewer workers want to work in dangerous jobs, so the equilibrium wage for high-risk jobs is usually higher.

(Continues on the next page.)

Lesson Vocabulary

derived demand a type of demand that is set by the demand for another good or service

equilibrium wage the wage rate, or price of labor services, that is set when the supply of workers meets the demand for workers in the labor market

unskilled labor labor that requires no specialized skills, education, or training

semi-skilled labor labor that requires minimal specialized skills and education

skilled labor labor that requires specialized abilities and training

professional labor labor that demands advanced skills and education

MODIFIED CORNELL NOTES

Still other factors play a role in setting wages. In the past, women and members of minority groups often received lower wages than white male workers performing the same jobs. In the 1960s, Congress outlawed wage discrimination based on gender or race. In spite of protections against discrimination, women still tend to earn less than men, and minorities tend to earn less than whites. The term **glass ceiling** refers to an unofficial and invisible barrier in some workplaces that prevents some women and minorities from advancing.

Wage levels are also affected by minimum wage laws, workplace safety laws, responses employers take to reduce wages, and labor unions. Because of minimum wage laws, employers may be forced to pay more than the equilibrium wage for unskilled labor. Safety laws that require an employer to make a workplace safer may mean that more workers are willing to work there. As the supply of workers increases, wages may decrease. Employers may also try to reduce their cost for wages by using machines instead of people or by outsourcing. Lastly, unions—organizations that promote the interests of workers—have an effect on wages because union members can negotiate for higher wages than nonunion workers in similar jobs.

Lesson Vocabulary

glass ceiling   an unofficial barrier that sometimes prevents some women and minorities from advancing to the top rank of organizations dominated by men

TOPIC 5 / LESSON 7

Lesson Summary
LABOR UNIONS

MODIFIED CORNELL NOTES

Labor unions are organized groups of workers that work to support the interest of their members with respect to wages, benefits, and working conditions. They use collective bargaining to extract concessions from employers. In recent times, shifts in the U.S. economy have caused a decline in union membership.

The labor union movement took shape over more than a century, and was largely a response to changes brought on by the Industrial Revolution. Facing dangerous conditions and long hours at factory jobs, workers began to form unions to protect their interests. The unions used **strikes**, or work stoppages, to force employers to address their demands. Laws at the time did not favor union organization, and the unions faced opposition from employers.

Samuel Gompers, an early leader in the U.S. labor movement, founded the American Federation of Labor in 1886. He focused on three reforms: higher wages, shorter hours, and safer work environments. In the 1930s, Congress passed measures that were more favorable to unions. Union membership increased, peaking in the 1940s.

As unions grew larger, some began to abuse their power. In 1947, in an effort to curb union power, Congress passed the Taft-Hartley Act, which allowed states to pass laws that banned mandatory union membership. These **right-to-work laws** were one of several factors that may have caused a decline in union membership. Another cause for the decline may be due to the fact that unions have traditionally been favored by **blue-collar workers** in manufacturing jobs. A decline in manufacturing activity has contributed to a decline in union membership. In addition, foreign competition has prompted some U.S. companies to lay off workers, which has further cut into union strength. Other factors contributing to the decline in union membership include foreign competition, automation, and the relocation of some businesses to the South, a region that has historically been less friendly to unions.

(Continues on the next page.)

Lesson Vocabulary

strike   an organized work stoppage intended to force an employer to address union demands

right-to-work law   a measure that bans mandatory union membership

blue-collar worker   a worker who performs manual labor, often in a manufacturing job, and earns an hourly wage

TOPIC 5 LESSON 7

Lesson Summary
LABOR UNIONS (continued)

In a company at which workers are represented by a union, management and labor periodically come together to negotiate employment contracts about issues such as wages and benefits, working conditions, and job security. This process of negotiating is called **collective bargaining**. If collective bargaining is not successful, the union members may vote to strike, a process that may be damaging to both labor and management. Sometimes the two sides agree to **mediation**, in which a third party is asked to find a solution both parties will accept. However, mediation is not binding. If mediation fails, labor and management may decide to use **arbitration**, in which the third party's decision is legally binding.

Lesson Vocabulary

collective bargaining   the process in which union and company management meet to negotiate a new labor contract

mediation   a settlement technique in which a neutral person, the mediator, meets with each side to try to find a solution that both sides will accept

arbitration   a settlement technique in which a neutral third party listens to both sides and then imposes a decision that is legally binding for both the company and the union

Name _____ Class _____ Date _____

Answer the questions below using the information in the Lesson Summaries on the previous pages.

Lesson 1: Sole Proprietorships

1. What are the advantages and disadvantages of sole proprietorships?

_____

_____

2. **Draw Inferences** Why do you think more than 70 percent of all businesses are organized as sole proprietorships?

_____

_____

Lesson 2: Partnerships and Franchises

3. What are the chief characteristics of a general partnership?

_____

_____

4. **Draw Inferences** Why do you think partnerships find it easier to obtain loans than sole proprietorships?

_____

_____

Lesson 3: Corporations

5. Describe the difference between stocks and bonds. Explain how each can benefit a corporation.

_____

_____

6. **Determine Central Ideas** Why can corporations exist longer than simple proprietorships or partnerships?

_____

_____

Lesson 4: Nonprofit Organizations

7. One of the principles of cooperatives is "voluntary and open membership." What do you think this means?

_____

_____

TOPIC 5

Review Questions

BUSINESS AND LABOR (continued)

8. **Draw Conclusions** If you were a cotton farmer, why might you choose to join a cooperative? What type would it be?

_____

_____

Lesson 5: The Labor Force

9. How are outsourcing and offshoring different?

_____

_____

10. **Draw Inferences** There are benefits to having only permanent employees at a company, and there are benefits to replacing such employees with temporary workers. Which do you think is better for a company. Why?

_____

_____

Lesson 6: Labor and Wages

11. Why is the demand for professional labor generally high relative to the supply compared to the demand for unskilled or semi-skilled labor?

_____

_____

12. **Assess an Argument** Jonah is looking for a summer job. He decides that applying with the city to collect trash is likely to pay more money than working at the ice cream shop. Explain why his argument makes sense.

_____

_____

Lesson 7: Labor Unions

13. What are two factors that have caused labor union membership to decline significantly over the past 50 years?

_____

_____

14. **Draw Inferences** What do you think would have happened if unions hadn't formed?

_____

_____

TOPIC 6 — Note Taking Study Guide

MONEY, BANKING, AND FINANCIAL MARKETS

Focus Question: How can you make the most of your money?

As you read the Lesson Summaries on the following pages, take notes about how you can make the most of your money through the use of the financial organizations described in them.

Banks	Investment	Bonds and Other Assets	Stocks
•	•	•	•
•	•	•	•
•			
•			
•			
•			

TOPIC 6 LESSON 1 — Lesson Summary
THE ROLE OF MONEY

Money is anything that serves as a medium of exchange, a unit of account, and a store of value. A **medium of exchange** is anything used to measure value during the exchange of goods and services. As a **unit of account,** money is a way to compare the value of goods and services. Money can also be used as a **store of value**. This means money keeps its value if you hold on to it.

The coins and paper bills used as money in a society are called **currency**. Currency must have six characteristics: durability, portability, divisibility, uniformity, scarcity, and acceptability. It must have durability, or be able to withstand a lot of use. It must have portability, or be easily carried and transferred. It must be divisible, or easily divided into smaller units. It must have uniformity, meaning that people must be able to count and measure money accurately. Currency must exhibit scarcity, meaning it must have a controlled supply. Finally, it must have acceptability, the ability to be accepted by all people in society.

Different types of money are valuable for different reasons. **Commodity money** is made up of objects of value, such as precious stones, that are used as money. **Representative money** represents an object of value for which it can be exchanged. For example, paper receipts for gold or silver were an early form of representative money. The United States today uses **fiat money**. This type of money has value because the government states that it is an acceptable means to pay debts.

Lesson Vocabulary

money   anything that serves as a medium of exchange, a unit of account, and a store of value

medium of exchange   anything that is used to determine value during the exchange of goods and services

unit of account   a means for comparing the values of goods and services

store of value   to keep value when held onto or stored instead of spent

currency   anything used as money; today we use coins and paper bills as money

commodity money   consists of objects that have value in and of themselves and that are also used as money

representative money   makes use of objects that have value solely because the holder can exchange them for something else of value

fiat money   has value because a government has decreed that it is an acceptable means to pay debts

Name _____ Class _____ Date _____

MODIFIED CORNELL NOTES

A **bank** is an institution for receiving, keeping, and lending money. In 1791, Congress set up the Bank of the United States. It lent money to the federal government and issued bank notes, a form of representative money backed by gold and silver. The Bank brought stability to American banking. However, many people opposed it. They worried that a centralized bank would respond only to the needs of wealthy individuals and large businesses. It ceased to exist in 1811, when its charter, or license, expired. A second central bank had the same fate, expiring in 1836.

The period between 1837 and 1863 is known as the Free Banking Era. This period was dominated by state-chartered banks. Many of these banks did not have enough gold and silver to back their paper money. During the Civil War, Congress enacted important bank reforms. These laws gave the federal government the power to charter banks. Banks were now required to hold adequate gold and silver reserves. The government also established a uniform national currency.

In 1913, Congress established the Federal Reserve System. It served as the nation's first true **central bank**, or bank that can lend to other banks in times of need. In the 1930s, the severe economic decline called the Great Depression led to new laws regulating banks. One established the Federal Deposit Insurance Corporation (FDIC), which insures customer deposits if a bank fails.

In 2008, after banks had made too many high-risk loans to people who wanted to buy homes, banks faced a crisis. Many people could not repay these loans, which led to a large number of **foreclosures**. A foreclosure is when a bank takes a home away from its owner. The United States economy suffered as banks began lending less money, the economy slowed down, and many people lost their jobs.

Lesson Vocabulary

bank   an institution for receiving, keeping, and lending money

central bank   a bank that can lend to other banks in times of need

foreclosure   the seizure of property from borrowers who are unable to repay their loans

TOPIC 6 LESSON 3 — Lesson Summary
THE FEDERAL RESERVE SYSTEM

After a series of banking crises, Congress passed the Federal Reserve Act in 1913. The Federal Reserve System, often referred to as "the Fed," is a group of 12 regional independent banks. During the Great Depression, the regional banks did not always agree on what actions to take. In response, Congress reformed the Fed in 1935, giving it more centralized power to deal with crises such as the Great Depression.

Member banks own the Federal Reserve System. Members include all nationally-chartered banks, which are required to join, and some state-chartered banks, which may join if they wish. A Board of Governors, appointed by the President, oversees the Fed. To prevent the board from being influenced by politics, no one President may appoint all the governors. The President also appoints the Board's chair. The chair is the main spokesperson for the nation's **monetary policy,** the actions the Fed takes to influence the money supply.

The Federal Reserve System is divided into 12 regional Federal Reserve Districts, with one regional Federal Reserve Bank in each. They monitor and report on district economic and banking conditions. The Federal Open Market Committee (FOMC) makes key decisions about interest rates and the growth of the U.S. money supply. Its members are drawn from the Board of Governors and the 12 district banks.

The Fed provides banking services to the federal government. It maintains a checking account for the Treasury Department and processes payments, such as Social Security checks and IRS refunds. When the Treasury Department auctions government bonds, the funds gained from such sales are deposited into the Federal Reserve Bank of New York. The Fed also issues paper currency and takes worn or damaged bills out of circulation.

The Fed provides banking services to banks. One service is **check clearing,** the process by which banks record whose account gives up money and whose account receives money when someone writes a check. The Fed sends out bank examiners to supervise lending practices and other activities of member banks.

(Continues on the next page.)

Lesson Vocabulary

monetary policy   the actions that the Federal Reserve System takes to influence the level of real GDP and the rate of inflation in the economy

check clearing   the process by which banks record whose account gives up money and whose account receives money as a result of a customer writing a check

TOPIC 6
LESSON 3

Lesson Summary
THE FEDERAL RESERVE SYSTEM (continued)

Banks often lend each other money from their reserve balances. These funds are called federal funds. The interest rate that banks charge each other for these loans is called the **federal funds rate**. Banks can also borrow directly from the Federal Reserve.

The Federal Reserve is best known for its role in regulating the nation's money supply. The law of supply and demand affects money as well as the rest of the economy. Too much money in the economy leads to inflation. Ideally, the Fed tries to increase the money supply by the same rate as the growth in the demand for money.

Lesson Vocabulary

federal funds rate   the interest rate that banks can charge each other for loans

Name _____ Class _____ Date _____

MODIFIED CORNELL NOTES

The **money supply** is all the money available in the United States economy. The money supply is divided into categories called Ml and M2. Ml is money that people can easily use to pay for goods and services, such as currency and deposits in checking accounts. These are assets that have **liquidity,** which means they can be used as cash or easily turned into cash. M2 consists of all the assets in Ml plus several other assets that have less liquidity, such as savings accounts and **money market mutual funds**. These are funds that pool money from small investors to purchase government or corporate bonds.

The basic service banks provide is a safe way for people to store and save money. Banks offer savings accounts, checking accounts, money market accounts and certificates of deposit. Most of these accounts pay **interest,** the price paid for the use of borrowed money. Banks also provide loans, mortgages, and credit cards. A **mortgage** is a loan used for real estate. When banks lend money, they make a profit by charging interest. The borrower also has to repay the **principal,** the amount borrowed. **Credit cards** allow consumers to buy goods and services based on a promise to pay for them at a later date. Many of the loans that banks offer have positive aspects, such as convenience, but also have negative aspects, such as the fact that the interest on loans and credit cards can become costly over time.

Computers are rapidly changing the world of banking. Automated Teller Machines (ATMs) are computers that customers can use to deposit money, withdraw cash, and obtain information. Customers use **debit cards** to get cash from ATMs and to make purchases. Many people use the Internet to handle their finances. A growing number of financial institutions allow people to check account balances, transfer money between accounts, and pay their bills by computer.

Lesson Vocabulary

money supply   all the money available in the United States economy

liquidity   the ability to be used as, or directly converted into, cash

money market mutual fund   funds that pool money from small savers to purchase short-term government and corporate securities

interest   the price paid for the use of borrowed money

mortgage   a specific type of loan that is used to buy real estate

principal   the amount of money borrowed

credit card   a card entitling its owner to buy goods and services based on the owner's promise to pay for those goods and services

debit card   a card used to withdraw money from a bank account

MODIFIED CORNELL NOTES

Investment promotes economic growth. **Investment** is the act of redirecting resources from being used today so that they can create future benefits. The **financial system** makes investment possible by allowing the transfer of money between savers and borrowers. Savers are households and businesses that lend out their savings. Borrowers are governments and businesses that use the money they borrow to build roads, factories, and homes. Borrowers may also use these funds to develop new products or provide new services.

Financial intermediaries are institutions that help channel funds from savers to borrowers. Examples include banks and **mutual funds,** funds that pool savings from many people and invest this money in different ways. Other financial intermediaries are pension funds, life insurance companies, and hedge funds. **Hedge funds** are private investment organizations that offer riskier investments with the potential for larger profits.

Financial intermediaries provide three major advantages to investors. They reduce risk by helping people invest in a variety of opportunities. The idea of spreading out investments to reduce risk is called **diversification**. Financial intermediaries also provide information and liquidity to investors.

Saving and investing involves trade-offs. For example, savings accounts have very low risk, and are liquid, but they also have a low return. **Return** is the money, such as interest, an investor receives above and beyond the sum of money initially invested. An investment with higher risk or less liquidity usually offers a higher potential return. Investors will be more tempted to take on more risk or to give up liquidity if they have a chance of earning more money on their investment.

Lesson Vocabulary

investment   the act of redirecting resources from being consumed today so that they may create benefits in the future; the use of assets to earn income or profit

financial system   the network of structures and mechanisms that allows the transfer of money between savers and borrowers

financial intermediary   an institution that helps channel funds from savers to borrowers

mutual fund   an organization that pools the savings of many individuals and invests this money in a variety of stocks, bonds, and other financial assets

hedge fund   a private investment organization that employs risky strategies that often make huge profits for investors

diversification   the strategy of spreading out investments to reduce risk

return   the money an investor receives above and beyond the sum of money initially invested

Name _____ Class _____ Date _____

Lesson Summary
BONDS AND OTHER FINANCIAL ASSETS

MODIFIED CORNELL NOTES

Bonds are loans that the government or a corporation must repay to an investor. Bonds usually pay a fixed amount of interest at regular intervals for a set amount of time. At **maturity,** the end of that period, the issuer repays the **par value,** or the original amount of investment, to the bondholder.

Investors like bonds because they are good investments and usually have low risk. However, because bonds are low-risk investments, their returns are often less than those of other investments. Issuers like bonds because once the bond is sold, interest rates on that bond will not go up or down. However, issuers must make fixed interest payments and repay the principal when due, even in bad years.

There are several types of bonds. **Savings bonds** are issued by the United States government. The United States Treasury Department issues treasury bonds, and state and local governments and municipalities issue **municipal bonds**. Interest on government-issued bonds is exempt from certain taxes. Corporations sell **corporate bonds** to raise money to expand their businesses.

Other types of financial assets include certificates of deposit (CDs) and mutual funds. Markets for financial assets are often classified according to the length of time for which funds are lent. **Capital markets** are markets in which money is lent for longer than a year. **Money markets** are markets in which money is lent for less than a year.

Lesson Vocabulary

maturity   the time at which payment to a bondholder is due

par value   a bond's stated value, to be paid to the bondholder at maturity

savings bond   a low-denomination bond issued by the United States government

municipal bond   a bond issued by a state or local government or a municipality to finance a public project

corporate bond   a bond issued by a corporation to help raise money for expansion

capital market   a market in which money is lent for periods longer than a year

money market   a market in which money is lent for periods of one year or less

Name _____ Class _____ Date _____

MODIFIED CORNELL NOTES

By selling stock, corporations raise the money that is necessary to start their businesses and keep them growing. Investors in stocks may make a profit in two ways: by receiving a dividend, a payment made by corporations to stockholders; and by selling the stock for more than they paid for it. The difference in price is called a **capital gain**. However, purchasing stock is risky. The stock price may decrease. Investors who sell their stock for less than they paid for it experience a **capital loss**.

The portions of stock that people buy are called **shares** of stock. These shares are bought and sold in markets called **stock exchanges**. When people talk about "the stock market" they usually mean the New York Stock Exchange (NYSE), one of the largest in the country. The performance of the NYSE is often measured by the performance of the few stocks included in the Dow Jones Industrial Average, or "The Dow." When the stock market rises steadily over a period of time, a **bull market** exists. When it falls for a period of time, people call it a **bear market**.

During the bull market of the 1920's, there was a great amount of **speculation,** high-risk investment with borrowed money in hope of big returns. This period ended in the stock market collapse called the "Great Crash" of October 1929. Another bull market occurred in the 1990s and ended in 2000. In the first decade of the twenty-first century, the stock market had a great deal of turmoil, with several significant gains and losses.

Lesson Vocabulary

capital gain   the difference between the selling price and purchase price that results in a financial gain for the seller

capital loss   the difference between the selling price and purchase price that results in a financial loss for the seller

share   a portion of stock

stock exchange   a market for buying and selling stock

bull market   a steady rise in stock prices in general over a period of time

bear market   a steady drop or stagnation in stock prices in general over a period of time

speculation   the practice of making high-risk investments with borrowed money in hopes of getting a big return

Answer the questions below using the information in the Lesson Summaries on the previous pages.

Lesson 1: The Role of Money

1. Name and give examples of two of the three functions of money. (Do not cite examples provided in the Lesson.)

_____

_____

2. Draw Conclusions Explain why cattle would not be good to use as money today.

_____

_____

Lesson 2: Changes in American Banking

3. Read the first paragraph of the lesson summary. What do you think the word *backed* means?

_____

_____

4. Draw Inferences Why do you think the period between 1837 and 1863 was known as the Free Banking Era?

_____

_____

Lesson 3: The Federal Reserve System

5. What is the relationship between the Fed and the Treasury?

_____

_____

6. Draw Inferences Where do the income tax payments that the Treasury receives go?

_____

_____

Lesson 4: The Functions of Modern Banks

7. What is the main difference between M1 and M2?

_____

_____

8. Draw Conclusions Why would a person want assets with liquidity?

_____

_____

TOPIC
6

Review Questions
MONEY, BANKING, AND FINANCIAL MARKETS (continued)

Lesson 5: Investing
9. Why is diversification important to have in investments?

_____

_____

10. Draw Inferences Would it be better to lend your money to a bank at a 2 percent interest rate or to a friend at a 4 percent interest rate? Explain your answer.

_____

_____

Lesson 6: Bonds and Other Financial Assets
11. If a business wanted to construct a new office building, replace all its equipment, and hire new employees, what type of bond would it issue?

_____

_____

12. Draw Inferences Why do you think government bonds usually have a low risk of default?

_____

_____

Lesson 7: Stocks
13. Why do corporations sell stocks?

_____

_____

14. Explain an Argument Do you think the benefits of investing in stock outweigh the risks? Why or why not?

_____

_____

_____

Name _____ Class _____ Date _____

Focus Question: Why should we care how the economy is doing?

As you read the Lesson Summaries on the following pages, think about why it is important for people to care about how the economy is doing and take notes in the following chart summarizing the content of this section.

Economic Measures	Business Cycles
•	•
•	•
•	•
•	•

Economic Growth and Contraction	Unemployment and Poverty
•	•
•	•
•	•
•	•

Name _____ Class _____ Date _____

MODIFIED CORNELL NOTES

Economists study economic performance using **national income accounting,** a system of collecting statistics on the economy. The U.S. Department of Commerce collects this data in the form of National Income and Products Accounts (NIPA).

The most important NIPA measure is **gross domestic product (GDP),** the dollar value of all final goods and services produced in a country's borders in a given year. GDP does not include **intermediate goods,** goods used to produce final goods. For example, the price of a new house that is sold is included in GDP, but not the nails and lumber used to build that house. GDP includes goods produced in the country by a foreign company, but not goods that an American company produces in another country.

When the GDP is expressed in current prices it called current GDP or **nominal GDP**. Changing prices, however, can distort nominal GDP. To correct this, economists determine **real GDP,** GDP expressed in constant, or unchanging, prices.

Another important NIPA measure is **gross national product (GNP)**. GNP includes income earned by U.S. companies outside of the country, but does not include the income earned by foreign firms doing business in the country.

As you might expect, supply and demand affect GDP. Economists calculate the **price level,** the average of all prices, to determine **aggregate supply,** the amount of goods and services in the economy available at all possible price levels. **Aggregate demand** is the amount of goods and services in the economy that will be purchased at all possible price levels. The intersection of aggregate supply and aggregate demand on a graph indicates the equilibrium price level and real GDP of the economy.

Lesson Vocabulary

national income accounting   a system economists use to collect and organize macroeconomic statistics on production, income, investment, and savings

gross domestic product (GDP)   the dollar value of all final goods and services produced within a country s borders in a given year

intermediate goods   products used in the production of final goods

nominal GDP   GDP measured in current prices

real GDP   GDP expressed in constant, or unchanging, prices

gross national product (GNP)   the annual income earned by a nation's companies and people

price level   the average of all prices in an economy

aggregate supply   the total amount of goods and services in the economy available at all possible price levels

aggregate demand   the amount of goods and services in the economy that will be purchased at all possible price levels

Name _____ Class _____ Date _____

MODIFIED CORNELL NOTES

A **business cycle** is a period of economic expansion followed by a period of contraction. Business cycles are major changes in GDP above or below normal levels. Business cycles have four phases. **Expansion** is a period of economic growth, as measured by a rise in real GDP. The **peak** is the height of expansion, when real GDP stops rising. A **contraction,** a period of economic slowdown marked by falling real GDP, follows the peak. The **trough** is the contraction's lowest point, when real GDP stops falling. A contraction that lasts for at least six months is called a **recession**. A **depression** is a long and severe recession.

Business cycles are affected by four main factors: business –investment, interest rates and credit, consumer expectations, and unexpected external shocks. For example, increased business –investment usually leads to increased output and jobs, helping to increase GDP and expand the economy. However, a drop in business spending reduces output and income, which may lead to a decline in GDP. Economists study these factors in order to predict the next turn of the business cycle.

Economic activity in the United States has followed a pattern of cycles. The Great Depression, which began in 1929, was the most severe economic downturn. Since then there have been several recessions, including short ones in 1991 and 2001. A crisis in home mortgage lending and banking led to a severe recession that began in late 2007. Although the recession officially ended when GDP begin rising again in the middle of 2009, its effects, including unemployment, have been long-lasting.

Lesson Vocabulary

business cycle   a period of macroeconomic expansion followed by a period of macroeconomic contraction

expansion   a period of economic growth as measured by a rise in real GDP

peak   the height of an economic expansion

contraction   an economic decline marked by falling real GDP

trough   the lowest point in an economic contraction

recession   a prolonged economic contraction

depression   a deep recession with features such as high unemployment and low economic output

Lesson Summary
ECONOMIC GROWTH

MODIFIED CORNELL NOTES

The basic measure of a nation's economic growth rate is the percentage change of real GDP over a given period of time. A nation's population tends to grow. Real GDP must keep up with the population growth rate. The best measure of a nation's standard of living is **real GDP per capita.** That divides the nation's real GDP by the number of people it has (per capita means per person). Real GDP per capita lets economists compare economies for different time periods and different nations.

Physical capital contributes to an economy's output and aids economic growth. **Capital deepening** is the process of increasing the amount of capital, such as machinery or tools, per worker. It is an important source of economic growth in modern economies. Increases in human capital also lead to economic growth. Better educated workers can produce more output per hour of work.

An economy increases its capital through saving and investment. **Saving** is income that consumers do not spend to purchase goods and services. Money that is saved, which may be held in a bank, is then available for investment. The **savings rate** is the proportion of disposable income spent to income saved. In the long run, a higher savings rate means more growth in real GDP. Government actions, such as raising or lower taxes, can affect how much money people have available for savings and investment.

Besides capital deepening, the other key source of economic growth is **technological progress.** This is an increase in efficiency gained by producing more output without using more inputs. Scientific research, innovation, larger markets, more natural resources, and improved education can all be sources of technological progress.

Lesson Vocabulary

real GDP per capita   real GDP divided by the total population of a country

capital deepening   the process of increasing the amount of capital per worker

saving   income not used for consumption

savings rate   the proportion of disposable income that is saved

technological progress   an increase in efficiency gained by producing more output without using more inputs

TOPIC 7 LESSON 4

Lesson Summary
UNEMPLOYMENT

Economists examine four kinds of unemployment. **Frictional unemployment** occurs when people are in between jobs or returning to the work force after a period of not working. **Seasonal unemployment** occurs in industries that slow or shut down for a particular time of the year, such as after a harvest or a busy holiday season. **Structural unemployment** happens when workers' skills do not match the jobs that are available. For example, new technology may cost jobs in industries that rely on older ways of producing goods. **Cyclical unemployment** occurs during recessions, when the demand for goods and services drops. The resulting slowdown in production causes the demand for labor to drop, and companies lay off employees.

One cause of structural unemployment is **globalization,** which is an increase in trade and other business connections around the world. As a result of globalization, companies sometimes move jobs to countries where costs are lower. That can lead to a loss of certain types of jobs, which increases structural unemployment.

The amount of unemployment is an important clue to the health of the nation's economy. The federal government tracks the **unemployment rate,** or the percentage of the nation's labor force that is unemployed. To determine the unemployment rate, the Bureau of Labor Statistics polls a large sample of the population every month.

(Continues on the next page.)

Lesson Vocabulary

frictional unemployment   type of unemployment that occurs when people take time to find a job

seasonal unemployment   type of unemployment that occurs as a result of harvest schedules, vacations, or when industries make seasonal shifts in their production schedules

structural unemployment   type of unemployment that occurs when workers skills do not match those needed for the jobs available

cyclical unemployment   unemployment that rises during economic downturns and falls when the economy improves

globalization   the increasingly tight interconnection of producers, consumers, and financial systems around the world

unemployment rate   the percentage of a nation's labor force that is unemployed

TOPIC **7** LESSON 4	**Lesson Summary**
	UNEMPLOYMENT (continued)

Since frictional, seasonal, and structural employment occur even in an economy that is working properly, economists expect some unemployment. An unemployment rate of 4 to 6 percent is considered **full employment,** the level of employment reached when there is no cyclical unemployment. However, some people with jobs are **underemployed,** meaning that they work part time when they want full-time jobs, or work at jobs that are below their skills.

Lesson Vocabulary

full employment   the level of employment reached when there is no cyclical unemployment

underemployed   working at a job for which one is overqualified, or working part time when full-time work is desired

TOPIC 7 LESSON 5	**Lesson Summary**
	INFLATION AND DEFLATION

MODIFIED CORNELL NOTES

Inflation is a general increase in prices. In a period of inflation, as prices rise, the same amount of money buys less. Inflation reduces people's **purchasing power,** their ability to buy goods and services. To track inflation, economists use a **price index,** a measurement that shows how the average price of a standard group of goods changes over time. The best known index is the **Consumer Price Index (CPI).** The CPI measures the prices of a **market basket,** which is a representative collection of goods and services used by a typical urban consumer. Economists calculate the change in the CPI from year to year to determine the **inflation rate,** the percentage change in prices over time.

Economists offer three reasons for why inflation begins. The **quantity theory** states that too much money in the economy leads to inflation. Another theory is that inflation occurs when demand for goods and services exceeds existing supplies. A third theory states that inflation occurs when producers raise prices in order to meet increased costs for labor and raw materials. This situation can lead to a **wage-price spiral,** which occurs when increases in one type of prices can cause other prices to rise, and the cycle then continues.

Typically, when unemployment falls to very low levels, inflation tends to increase. The supply of available workers shrinks and employers have to offer higher wages to attract workers. Inflation is especially hard on people living on a **fixed income,** such as Social Security payments, which does not rise as other wages and prices rise.

In the early 2000s, the economy had a period of slow growth. Some economists predicted a period of **deflation,** or a sustained drop in the price level. The economy recovered, however, and inflation remained low.

Lesson Vocabulary

inflation   a general increase in prices across an economy

purchasing power   the ability to purchase goods and services

price index   a measurement that shows how the average price of a standard group of goods changes over time

Consumer Price Index (CPI)   a price index determined by measuring the price of a standard group of goods meant to represent the market basket of a typical urban consumer

market basket   a representative collection of goods and services

inflation rate   the percentage rate of change in price level over time

quantity theory   the theory that too much money in the economy causes inflation

wage-price spiral   the process by which rising wages cause higher prices, and higher prices cause higher wages

fixed income   income that does not increase even when prices go up

deflation   a sustained drop in the price level

Name _____ Class _____ Date _____

MODIFIED CORNELL NOTES

The government defines a poor family as one whose total income is less than the amount needed to satisfy minimal needs. The U.S. Census Bureau determines the **poverty threshold,** the income level below that which is needed to support a household or family. This threshold varies with family size. In 2013, the threshold was $15,510 for a single parent under age 65 with one child. The threshold was $23,550 for a family of four with two children. The poverty rate is the percentage of people who live in households below the poverty threshold. The **poverty rate** varies among different groups. Among African Americans or Latinos Native Americans, it is more than twice as high as for white Americans.

The causes of poverty include unemployment, lack of education, and discrimination based on race and gender. Many poor people live in areas such as inner cities or isolated rural areas, where there are few high-paying jobs. Other causes of poverty include economic slowdowns and the increasing number of single-parent families.

The United States has millions of poor people, but it also has the world's highest per capital GDP. This is because **income distribution,** the way income is distributed among the population, is unequal. The richest 20 percent of the population earns income more than rest of the population combined. The government spends billions of dollars on programs designed to reduce poverty. **Enterprise zones,** for example, are low-employment areas where companies can locate free of certain taxes. State and federal governments also provide **cash transfers,** which are direct payments of money to poor, disabled, or retired people.

In addition to government actions, many private groups also work to decrease poverty and help people living in poverty. The government encourages these actions by allowing people to take tax deductions for charitable contributions.

Lesson Vocabulary

poverty threshold an income level below that which is needed to support families or households

poverty rate the percentage of people who live in households with income below the official poverty line

income distribution the way in which a nation's total income is distributed among its population

enterprise zones an area where businesses can locate free of certain local, state, and federal taxes and restrictions

cash transfers direct payments of money by the government to people who are poor, disabled, or retired

TOPIC 7 — Review Questions
ECONOMIC PERFORMANCE AND CHALLENGES

Answer the questions below using the information in the Lesson Summaries on the previous pages.

Lesson 1: Gross Domestic Product

1. What is the difference between nominal GDP and real GDP?

_____

_____

2. **Cite Evidence** Explain how buying a shirt contributes to the GDP. Relate it to all four parts of the definition of GDP: dollar value, final goods and services, produced within a country's borders, and in a given year.

_____

_____

Lesson 2: Business Cycles

3. How do economists differentiate between a recession and a depression?

_____

_____

4. **Draw Inferences** Why do you think economists can be certain that every expansion in the economy will be followed by a peak and then a contraction?

_____

_____

Lesson 3: Economic Growth

5. Explain in your own words what "real GDP per capita" means. Why do we need the "per capita" part to measure growth?

_____

_____

6. **Make Inferences** Does a rising GDP benefit everyone? Explain.

_____

_____

Lesson 4: Unemployment

7. What are the four different kinds of unemployment and the characteristics of each?

_____

_____

8. **Draw Conclusions** Why does an economy that has full employment have frictional, seasonal, and structural unemployment but not cyclical unemployment?

_____

_____

TOPIC 7 Review Questions
ECONOMIC PERFORMANCE AND CHALLENGES (continued)

Lesson 5: Inflation and Deflation

9. How are the CPI and the rate of inflation related? Explain how the CPI affects the rate of inflation.

_____

_____

10. **Draw Conclusions** How are most people likely to adjust their spending when prices for consumer goods are rising?

_____

_____

Lesson 6: Poverty and Income Distribution

11. What are the most recognized causes of poverty?

_____

_____

12. **Draw Conclusions** Is it possible for someone to work full time and still be poor?

_____

_____

Name _____ Class _____ Date _____

Focus Question: How do governments at different levels spend the money they take in through taxes?

As you read the Lesson Summaries, take notes in the following chart to compare the way governments at the federal, state, and local levels raise and spend money.

	Federal	State/Local
Spending		
Taxes		

Name _____ Class _____ Date _____

MODIFIED CORNELL NOTES

Taxes are payments that people are required to pay to a local, state, or national government. Taxes supply revenue, or income, to provide the goods and services that people expect from government.

The Constitution grants and also limits the taxing power of Congress. The Constitution states that federal taxes must be used "to pay the debts and provide for the common defense and general welfare of the United States." A tax must be the same in all states, and may not be placed on exports. The Sixteenth Amendment, ratified in 1913, gave Congress the power to levy an income tax.

When government creates a tax, it decides on the **tax base**—the income, property, good, or service that is subject to a tax. It also decides how to structure the tax. The three basic kinds of tax structures are proportional, progressive, and regressive. A **proportional tax** is a tax in which the percentage of income paid in taxes remains the same for all income levels. A **progressive tax** is one in which the percentage of income paid in taxes increases as income increases. An example is the federal **individual income tax,** the tax levied on a person's income. This tax has several tax brackets, so incomes above certain levels are subject to higher tax rates than those below. In a **regressive tax,** the percentage of income paid in taxes increases as income goes down. A **sales tax,** a tax on the value of a good or service being sold, is generally regressive because higher-income people usually pay a lower proportion of their incomes on goods and services subject to the tax.

Lesson Vocabulary

taxes   a required payment to a local, state, or national government

tax base   the income, property, good, or service that is subject to a tax

proportional tax   a tax for which the percentage of income paid in taxes remains the same at all income levels

progressive tax   a tax for which the percentage of income paid in taxes increases as income increases

individual income tax   a tax based on a person's earnings

regressive tax   a tax for which the percentage of income paid in taxes decreases as income increases

sales tax   a tax based on goods or services that are sold

TOPIC 8 LESSON 2	Lesson Summary
	FEDERAL TAXES

The federal government has several sources of income. The largest is the individual income tax, which provides nearly half of federal tax receipts. It is collected on a "pay-as-you-earn" system throughout the year, mostly by employers **withholding,** or taking out part of an employee's income and sending it to the federal government. At the end of the year, taxpayers fill out a **tax return,** a form in which they declare all income and figure out their total tax. Depending on how much was withheld, the taxpayer may get a refund or owe additional taxes.

Taxable income is a person's gross, or total, income minus exemptions and deductions. Gross income includes income from salaries, wages, tips, and commissions, as well as from interest on savings accounts and stock dividends. **Personal exemptions** are set amounts that can be subtracted from gross income for the taxpayer and each family member. **Tax deductions** are certain expenses or payments made by a taxpayer that can deducted from gross income, including interest paid on a mortgage, donations to charity, and state and local tax payments. Some taxpayers may receive **tax credits,** which is an amount taken directly off a person's total tax. For example, people may get a tax credit for some child care expenses or tuition payments.

Corporations pay a corporate income tax on their income. The corporate income tax makes up about 11 percent of federal receipts. Like personal income taxes, corporate income tax rates increase as profits increase.

(Continues on the next page.)

Lesson Vocabulary

withholding   taking tax payments out of an employee's pay before he or she receives it

tax return   a form used to file income taxes

taxable income   the earnings on which tax must be paid; total income minus exemptions and deductions

personal exemptions   a set amount that taxpayers may subtract from their gross income for themselves, their spouse, and any dependents

tax deductions   a variable amount that taxpayers may subtract from their gross income

tax credits   a variable amount that taxpayers may subtract from the total amount of their income tax

Name _____ Class _____ Date _____

MODIFIED CORNELL NOTES

The Federal Insurance Contributions Act, or FICA, taxes are also withheld from people's paychecks. FICA taxes fund Social Security, which was established in 1935 as a retirement fund for workers. Now it also provides benefits to wage earners' surviving family members and people with disabilities. FICA taxes also fund Medicare, a national health insurance program for people over age 65 and those with certain disabilities.

There are several other types of federal taxes that bring relatively little revenue. These include the **estate tax,** which is a tax on the total value of a deceased person's estate, and the **gift tax** on money or property a living person gives to another.

Lesson Vocabulary

estate tax   a tax on the total value of the money and property of a person who has died

gift tax   a tax on the money or property that one living person gives to another

TOPIC
8
LESSON 3

Lesson Summary
FEDERAL SPENDING

The federal government spends nearly four trillion dollars a year. About two thirds of its spending, however, is "mandatory." **Mandatory spending** is money lawmakers are required by law to spend in certain amounts for certain programs and for interest payments on the national debt.

Most mandatory spending is for **entitlements,** which are benefits to which anyone who meets the program requirements is entitled by law. Spending on entitlement programs rises as the number of eligible people rises. The largest entitlement programs are Social Security, Medicare, and Medicaid, which provides health insurance to low-income families. Other mandatory spending programs include the Supplemental Nutrition Assistance Program and the National School Lunch Program. Mandatory spending also includes retirement benefits and insurance for federal workers, veterans' pensions, and unemployment benefits.

Discretionary spending is spending for which government can make choices. It accounts for about a third of federal spending. Discretionary spending includes defense spending, education, national parks and monuments, transportation, disaster aid, foreign aid, and many other items. The federal government also provides aid to state and local governments and shares the costs for some programs with them. Examples include highway construction and low-income housing.

Lesson Vocabulary

mandatory spending spending that Congress is required by existing law to do

entitlements social welfare programs that people are "entitled to" benefit from if they meet certain eligibility requirements

discretionary spending spending about which Congress is free to make choices

TOPIC 8 LESSON 4

Lesson Summary
STATE AND LOCAL TAXES AND SPENDING

State governments prepare two **budgets,** or estimates of future revenues and expenses. The **operating budget** pays day-to day expenses, such as salaries of state employees and computers for offices. The **capital budget** pays for major capital, or investment, spending. New bridges and buildings are examples of capital spending. Most states have laws requiring a **balanced budget**—a budget in which revenue is equal to spending. This rule applies only to the operating budget.

While tax policies and spending differ among states, most spend the largest amounts on education, public safety, highways, and public welfare. Public safety includes state police, crime labs, and corrections systems. States also build and maintain highways and roads, often with federal assistance. They support health and welfare programs and maintain parks and recreation facilities. States get revenue several ways. All but five states have a sales tax. States may also have excise taxes, state income taxes, taxes on **real property,** such as land and buildings, and **personal property,** such as furniture and jewelry. Most states collect corporate income taxes and license fees.

Local governments—towns, cities, townships, counties, and special districts—also collect taxes. These taxes support public schools, law enforcement, fire protection, libraries, airports, public hospitals, parks, public transportation, and more. The main source of local revenue is property taxes, a tax on the value of a property. Property taxes are paid by people who own homes, apartments, buildings, or land. An official called a **tax assessor** determines the value of the property. Local governments may also levy sales taxes, excise taxes, and income taxes.

Lesson Vocabulary

budget   an estimate of future revenue and expenses

operating budget   a budget for day-to-day spending needs

capital budget   a budget for spending on major investments

balanced budget   a budget in which revenue and spending are equal

real property   land and any permanent structures on the land to which a person has legal title

personal property   movable possessions or assets

tax assessor   an official who determines the value of property

Name _____ Class _____ Date _____

<table>
<tr><td>TOPIC
8</td><td>Review Questions
TAXES AND SPENDING</td></tr>
</table>

Answer the questions below using the information in the Lesson Summaries on the previous pages.

Lesson 1: Understanding Taxes

1. Use context clues about the nature of progressive taxes to come up with a definition of the word *progressive*.

_____

_____

2. Compare and Contrast How are progressive, proportional, and regressive taxes similar? How are they different?

_____

_____

Lesson 2: Federal Taxes

3. What are some steps a person can take to reduce his or her taxable income?

_____

_____

4. Determine Central Ideas Identify the common purpose of Social Security and Medicare taxes.

_____

_____

Lesson 3: Federal Spending

5. What is the difference between mandatory and discretionary spending?

_____

_____

6. Draw Conclusions Why do you think that the percentage of federal spending that is mandatory has grown in recent years?

_____

_____

Name _____ Class _____ Date _____

TOPIC 8 Review Questions
TAXES AND SPENDING (continued)

Lesson 4: State and Local Taxes and Spending

7. Suppose your state wanted to build a new public hospital to serve a rural area. From which budget—operating or capital—would this project be funded? Explain your answer.

_____

_____

8. **Draw Conclusions** Why does every state support at least one public university? What benefit does the state receive from this expense?

_____

_____

Name _____ Class _____ Date _____

Focus Question: What is the role of government in the economy?

As you read the Lesson Summaries that follow, take notes on the role the government plays in the economy by summarizing the contents of each Lesson in this chart.

Federal Budget and Fiscal Policy	Fiscal Policy Options	National Debt and Deficits	Monetary Policy
•	•	•	•
•	•	•	•
•	•	•	•
•	•	•	•

Name _____ Class _____ Date _____

MODIFIED CORNELL NOTES

Fiscal policy is the government's use of taxing and spending to influence the nation's economy. Decisions about fiscal policy are used to create the **federal budget,** a written document showing how much money the government expects to receive and spend in a year.

The budget process begins when each federal agency estimates spending for the next year. They send these estimates to the Office of Management and Budget (OMB), which is part of the executive branch. The OMB reviews proposals and works with the President's staff, who may make changes to these estimates. These estimates are then combined into one document, which the President presents to Congress. Congress reviews the budget with help from the Congressional Budget Office. Congress then proposes its modified budget and authorizes specific spending in **appropriations bills**. The President can sign these bills into law. The President can also veto the bills and seek additional changes.

Expansionary policies are designed to increase economic output. When the government increases its spending it buys more goods and services, leading to economic growth. When government cuts taxes, people have more money to spend, a situation that also leads to economic growth. Policies intended to decrease output are **contractionary policies**. These policies allow government to decrease its spending or raise taxes, both of which will lead to slower economic growth.

Fiscal policy is not easy to put into practice. Neither the Congress nor the President can change many parts of the budget. Also, the behavior of the economy is not easy to predict. During the time it takes to pass a budget and put a fiscal policy in place, the business cycle may change on its own. Also, changes to fiscal policy are not always popular.

Lesson Vocabulary

fiscal policy   the use of government spending and revenue collection to influence the economy

federal budget   a written document estimating the federal government's revenue and authorizing its spending for the coming year

appropriations bills   a bill that authorizes a specific amount of spending by the government

expansionary policies   a fiscal policy used to encourage economic growth, often through increased spending or tax cuts

contractionary policies   a fiscal policy used to reduce economic growth, often through decreased spending or higher taxes

Name _____ Class _____ Date _____

MODIFIED CORNELL NOTES

Classical economics is a school of thought stating that markets regulate themselves and will recover from ups and downs on their own. The Great Depression challenged this view. During the Depression, the economy did not recover quickly. Prices fell but demand did not increase because so many people lacked jobs and money. John Maynard Keynes introduced a theory about the economy, now called **Keynesian economics,** which encouraged a greater role for government in the economy. Keynes said the Depression lasted because neither consumers nor businesses had an incentive to increase spending. Companies would not increase production if consumers had no jobs and no money to buy their products. Keynes argued that the government could buy more goods and services, encouraging production, which in turn would put more people back to work.

Fiscal policy is powerful because of the **multiplier effect,** the idea that a dollar change in fiscal policy can have several times that impact on the economy. For example, if the government buys $10 billion in goods and services, GDP may increase by much more than $10 billion. This effect occurs because firms spend the $10 billion on wages, raw materials, and investment. The people who receive this money also spend it, creating more economic activity.

Supply-side economics argue that a better way to encourage economic activity is to lower taxes and put more money in people's pockets. People will then use the money to make investments and create jobs.

In recent times, both Keynesian and supply-side economics have won favor. Keynesian economics dominated the decades following World War II. Then, under President Ronald Reagan in the 1980s, the government implemented supply-side policies. A recession that started in 2007 seems to have introduced a return to Keynesian principles.

Lesson Vocabulary

classical economics   a school of thought based on the idea that free markets regulate themselves

Keynesian economics   a school of thought that uses demand-side theory as the basis for encouraging government action to help the economy

multiplier effect   the idea that every one-dollar change in fiscal policy creates a change greater than one dollar in the national income

supply-side economics   a school of thought based on the idea that the supply of goods drives the economy

TOPIC 9 LESSON 3

Lesson Summary
THE NATIONAL DEBT AND DEFICITS

When government revenues equal spending, a balanced budget exists. In reality, the federal budget is rarely balanced. A **budget surplus** occurs when annual revenues are higher than spending. A **budget deficit** occurs when spending is higher than revenues. In recent decades, deficits have occurred nearly every year.

When the government runs a deficit, it must find a way to pay for the extra expenditures. It can either create money or borrow money. Covering deficits by creating money can lead to high inflation. The main way that government deals with deficits is by borrowing money. Government borrows money mainly by selling bonds, such as United States Savings Bonds.

When government borrows money, it adds to the **national debt**, the total amount of money the government owes to bondholders. Two problems arise from a national debt. First, it reduces money available for businesses to borrow and invest because people buy government bonds instead of investing in business. This is called the **crowding-out effect**, because government borrowing crowds out, or forces out, private economic activity. Second, government pays interest to bondholders, and money spent paying interest cannot be spent elsewhere.

In the 1980s, huge deficits led Congress to pass laws cutting federal spending. After the Supreme Court found many of these laws unconstitutional, some people suggested amending the Constitution to require a balanced budget. Opponents said an amendment would prevent government from dealing with rapid economic changes.

At the end of the twentieth century, budget surpluses occurred for the first time in 30 years. However, war, tax cuts, and recession soon brought new deficits.

Lesson Vocabulary

budget surplus a situation in which budget revenues exceed expenditures

budget deficit a situation in which budget expenditures exceed revenues

national debt the total amount of money the federal government owes to bondholders

crowding-out effect the loss of funds for private investment caused by government borrowing

MODIFIED CORNELL NOTES

TOPIC 9 LESSON 4

Lesson Summary
MONETARY POLICY OPTIONS

Money enters the economy by a process called **money creation**. Banks create money by making loans of money people deposit in the bank. So, if a person deposits $1,000 in a bank, the bank can loan out most of that money to someone else. That loan will eventually wind up in a bank account, and most of that will be loaned out to another borrower. In this way, the original $1,000 deposit leads to the creation of hundreds of additional dollars in the economy.

The Fed has three tools for adjusting the amount of money in the economy. The simplest is to change the **reserve requirement ratio**, the amount of each bank deposit that a bank must keep in reserve and not lend out to another borrower. Reducing the ratio means that banks can lend out more money, increasing the money supply. Increasing the ratio has the opposite effect. This tool is rarely used today.

A second tool is to adjust the **discount rate**, which is the rate the Fed charges on loans to banks and other financial institutions. When the discount rate goes up or down, interest rates for other types of loans also go up or down. For example, a drop in the discount rate would generally lower the **prime rate**, which is the interest rate banks charge their best customers. When banks lend money at a lower rate, it tends to increase the overall money supply. Today, the Fed generally relies on changing the discount rate as part of its monetary policy.

(Continues on the next page.)

Lesson Vocabulary

money creation   the process by which money enters into circulation

reserve requirement ratio   the fraction of deposits that banks are required to keep in reserve

discount rate   the interest rate that the Federal Reserve charges commercial banks for loans

prime rate   the interest rate banks charge on short-term loans to their best customers

TOPIC 9 LESSON 4

Lesson Summary

MONETARY POLICY OPTIONS (continued)

MODIFIED CORNELL NOTES

The Fed's third and most commonly used monetary policy tool is **open market operations**, the buying and selling of government **securities** such as bonds. When the Fed wants to increase the money supply, it purchases government securities. The bond seller deposits money from the sale into the bank, starting the money creation process. To decrease the money supply, the Fed sells government securities. The money paid for the bond is taken out of circulation, and reserves are reduced. Open market operations tend to affect the **federal funds rate**, which is the interest rate banks charge each other for loans. Changes in the federal funds rate can also affect rates available to businesses and individuals.

Lesson Vocabulary

open market operations   the buying and selling of government securities in order to alter the supply of money

security   a financial document, such as a stock certificate or bond, that represents ownership of corporate shares or the promise of repayment by a company or government

federal funds rate   the interest rate banks charge one another for loans

Name _____ Class _____ Date _____

MODIFIED CORNELL NOTES

Monetarism is the belief that the money supply is the most important factor in macroeconomic performance. Monetary policy alters the supply of money, which in turn affects interest rates. When the supply of money is low, the price of money—the interest rate—is high. When the supply of money is high, interest rates are low.

The Fed can use monetary policy to expand or contract the U.S. economy. An **easy money policy** is a monetary policy that increases the money supply. A larger money supply means lower interest rates, which in turn means more money for investment and a boost to the economy. By contrast, a **tight money policy** is a monetary policy that reduces the money supply by raising interest rates. Higher interest rates lower GDP.

Timing is essential in monetary policy. Good timing smooths out ups and downs in the business cycle. Bad timing can make the business cycle more severe. For example, an expansionary policy may take effect as the economy is beginning to expand on its own, leading to overexpansion and inflation.

An **inside lag** is the time it takes to implement a policy. The inside lag can limit the effectiveness of monetary policy because it takes time to recognize a problem. An **outside lag** is the time it takes for the policy to take effect. Outside lags can mean that a monetary policy's impact occurs at the wrong time. Because of lags and the difficulty of predicting the direction of the economy, it is difficult to use monetary policy effectively. Some recessions are short and correct themselves in time. Policy makers are more likely to want to intervene in the case of a long and severe recession.

Lesson Vocabulary

monetarism   the belief that the money supply is the most important factor in macroeconomic performance

easy money policy   a monetary policy that increases the money supply

tight money policy   a monetary policy that reduces the money supply

inside lag   the time it takes to implement monetary policy

outside lag   the time it takes for monetary policy to have an effect

TOPIC 9 Review Questions

FISCAL AND MONETARY POLICY

Answer the questions below using the information in the Lesson Summaries on the previous pages.

Lesson 1: The Federal Budget and Fiscal Policy

1. Using your own words, explain why you think the federal budget reflects the nation's priorities.

_____

_____

2. **Determine Central Ideas** Explain how you think fiscal policy works to expand or slow economic growth, achieve employment, and maintain price stability.

_____

_____

Lesson 2: Fiscal Policy Options

3. What was Keynes's solution for motivating businesses to increase production during the Great Depression?

_____

_____

4. **Determine Central Ideas** Faced with an economy falling into recession, what would supply-side economists likely encourage the government to do?

_____

_____

Lesson 3: The National Debt and Deficits

5. What explains the existence of a budget deficit?

_____

_____

6. **Determine Central Ideas** What is the difference between a budget deficit and the national debt?

_____

_____

Lesson 4: Monetary Policy Options

7. If the discount rate rose, would you expect the prime rate to rise or fall? Why?

_____

_____

8. **Draw Conclusions** How are the discount rate and the federal funds rate different?

_____

_____

Lesson 5: The Effects of Monetary Policy

9. If you have a savings account, how will higher interest rates affect your savings?

_____

_____

10. **Analyze Interactions** Suppose that you have been saving money for a down payment on a house. If interest rates fall, would you be more or less likely to buy a house? Explain your answer.

_____

_____

TOPIC 10 Note Taking Study Guide
TRADE, DEVELOPMENT, AND GLOBALIZATION

Focus Question: How might scarcity divide our world or bring it together?

As you read the Lesson Summaries in this Topic, take notes in the outline to help you determine the ways that scarcity leads to division or unity.

I. Trade

  A. Why nations trade

    1.

    2.

  B.

    1.

    2.

II. Development

  A.

    1.

    2.

  B. Barriers to development

    1.

    2.

III. Globalization

  A.

    1.

    2.

  B. Challenges of globalization

    1.

    2.

MODIFIED CORNELL NOTES

TOPIC 10 LESSON 1 — Lesson Summary
WHY NATIONS TRADE

Natural resources, human capital, and physical capital are unevenly distributed from country to country. Because countries differ so much in resources, they also differ in their ability to produce different goods and services. They will specialize in certain products that they can produce most efficiently. For example, coffee is grown more efficiently in warm areas like Central America than in other parts of the world. Because countries cannot efficiently produce everything their citizens need and want, they engage in trade.

A person or nation has an **absolute advantage** when it can make more of a certain good with a given amount of resources than another person or nation. **Comparative advantage** is the ability of one person or nation to produce a good at a lower opportunity cost than that of another person or nation. A nation has a comparative advantage in the product that it can produce most efficiently given all the products it could choose to produce. The **law of comparative advantage** states that nations are better off when they produce goods and services in which they have a comparative advantage. The money nations make from selling those goods and services can be used to buy the goods and services they cannot produce as efficiently.

An **export** is a good sent to another country for sale. An **import** is a good brought in from another country for sale. The United States exports more goods than any other country except China. The United States is also the world's top importer.

As countries specialize in certain products in which they have a comparative advantage, changes in employment patterns can occur. For example, in the 1970s, Japan gained a comparative advantage in producing automobiles. As the American automobile industry lost business, many American workers lost their jobs.

Lesson Vocabulary

absolute advantage   the ability to produce more of a given product using a given amount of resources

comparative advantage   the ability to produce a product most efficiently given all the other products that could be produced

law of comparative advantage   the principle that a nation is better off when it produces goods and services for which it has a comparative advantage

export   a good or service sent to another country for sale

import   a good or service brought in from another country for sale

TOPIC 10 LESSON 2

Lesson Summary
TRADE BARRIERS AND AGREEMENTS

Most countries have **trade barriers**—a means of preventing a foreign product or service from freely entering a country. One type of trade barrier is an **import quota,** a law limiting the amount of a good that can be imported. A voluntary export restraint is a limit a country imposes on itself on the amount of exports it ships to another country. A **tariff** is a tax on imported goods.

Trade barriers have both positive and negative effects. For example, United States tariffs will result in higher prices on imported cars. This helps American car makers compete. However, consumers then pay more for imported cars. American manufacturers might lose the incentive to become more efficient and make less expensive cars. **Trade wars** are another possible negative effect of trade restrictions. When one country restricts imports, its trading partner may try to use similar restrictions. Trade wars can result in less trade.

Protectionism is the use of trade restrictions to protect a nation's industries. The most basic argument for protectionism is that it protects workers in industries that would be hurt by less expensive imports from other countries.

Recent trends have been toward lowering trade barriers and increasing trade through international trade agreements. The World Trade Organization (WTO) negotiates agreements and resolves trade disputes. The United States entered into a treaty in 1993 called NAFTA, the North American Free Trade Agreement, which reduced trade barriers between the United States, Canada, and Mexico. Opinions for and against NAFTA continue. Some say that it has helped the U.S. economy grow. Others say that it has taken away jobs from U.S. workers.

A large corporation that sells goods and services throughout the world is a multinational. Multinationals benefit from free trade. For example, an automobile company might design its cars in the United States and import parts made in Asia to an assembly plant in Canada.

Lesson Vocabulary

trade barrier   a means of preventing a foreign product or service from freely entering a nation's territory

import quota   a set limit on the amount of a good that can be imported

tariff   a tax on imported goods

trade war   a cycle of escalating trade barriers

protectionism   the use of trade barriers to shield domestic industries from foreign competition

Name _____ Class _____ Date _____

MODIFIED CORNELL NOTES

Before you can spend money in a foreign country you have to exchange your U.S. dollars for the currency of that nation. The value of that currency in relation to your own is the **exchange rate**. Exchange rates go up and down daily. An increase in the value of a currency is called **appreciation**. When a nation's currency appreciates, its products become more expensive to other nations, leading to a decrease in its exports. However, its imports become cheaper and usually increase in number. The opposite happens with **depreciation**, a decrease in the value of a nation's currency.

The **foreign exchange market**, which is made up of banks and other financial institutions, helps companies and nations exchange currencies. The foreign exchange market makes international trade possible. The world's countries work together to compare and keep track of exchange rates. A **fixed exchange-rate system** keeps the value of currencies constant against one another. Some countries fix their exchange rate against the U.S. dollar or the Euro. Since 1973, the United States and many other governments have adopted a **flexible exchange-rate system**, which allows exchange rates to be determined by supply and demand. Some European countries, members of the European Union, use the same currency, called the Euro, and the same central bank.

The relationship between imports and exports is called **balance of trade**. Nations seek to maintain a balance of trade. That is, they hope the value of imports is roughly equal to the value of exports. A **trade surplus** occurs when a nation exports more than it imports. A **trade deficit** occurs when a nation imports more than it exports. The United States has had a large trade deficit since the mid-1990s.

Lesson Vocabulary

exchange rate the value of a nation's currency in relation to a foreign currency

appreciation an increase in the value of a currency

depreciation a decrease in the value of a currency

foreign exchange market system of financial institutions that facilitate the buying and selling of foreign currencies

fixed exchange-rate system a system in which governments try to keep the values of their currencies somewhat constant against one another

flexible exchange-rate system a system in which the exchange rate is determined by supply and demand

balance of trade the relationship between the value of a country's exports and the value of its imports

trade surplus a situation in which a nation exports more goods and services than it imports

trade deficit a situation in which a nation imports more goods and services than it exports

TOPIC 10 LESSON 4

Lesson Summary
DEVELOPMENT

There are big differences between prosperous nations in the world and poorer nations. **Development** is the process by which any nation improves its people's economic, political, and social well-being. A nation's level of development tells how well a nation is able to feed, clothe, and shelter its people. **Developed nations**, such as the United States, have a high average level of material well-being. Most nations are **less developed countries (LDCs)**, with low levels of material well-being.

One group of LDCs has made great progress toward developing their economies. These **newly industrialized countries (NICs)** include Mexico, Brazil, Saudi Arabia, South Korea, and several countries in Eastern Europe. Some NICs are rich in resources. Others have turned to manufacturing.

The primary measure of level of development is **per capita gross domestic product (per capita GDP)**— a nation's gross domestic product (GDP) divided by its total population. For example, both Spain and India have fairly high GDPs. However, India has many more people, so it has a much lower per capita GDP. Another way to measure development is the amount of energy, such as oil and gas, used per person. Most developed nations have high levels of **industrialization**, the extensive organization of an economy for the purpose of manufacture. Countries with a high level of industrialization use large amounts of oil and electricity. By contrast, most LDCs use less amounts of energy per person, since large numbers of people engage in **subsistence agriculture**. They raise only enough food to feed their families.

(Continues on the next page.)

Lesson Vocabulary

development   the process by which a nation improves the economic, political, and social well-being of its people

developed nations   a nation with a relatively high average level of material well-being

less developed country   a nation with a relatively low average level of material well-being

newly industrialized country   a less developed country that has made great progress toward developing its economy

per capita GDP   a nation's gross domestic product divided by its population

industrialization   the organization of an economy for the purpose of manufacturing goods

subsistence agriculture   level of farming in which a person raises only enough food to feed his or her family

Name _____ Class _____ Date _____

MODIFIED CORNELL NOTES

Other ways to measure development include the literacy, life expectancy, and infant mortality rates. The **literacy rate**, the proportion of people over age 15 that can read and write, is higher in developed countries. So is **life expectancy**, the average expected life span of an individual. The **infant mortality rate**, the number of deaths that occur in the first year of life per 1,000 births, is lower in developed countries.

Developed nations have similar characteristics. Levels of consumer spending on goods such as computers are high in developed nations. In most developed nations, agricultural output is high, but relatively few people work on farms. Since only a small portion of the labor force is needed in agriculture, more people are available to work in industry and services. Widespread use of technology increases the productivity of this workforce, too. Developed nations tend to be urban rather than rural and have a strong infrastructure including transportation and communication systems.

Less developed nations have similar characteristics, too. Unemployment rates are high in less developed countries, often around 20 percent. Consumer goods that are produced in LDCs are often shipped out of the country and sold in more developed nations. A less developed country has trouble educating its populace. Resources for schools are limited. In the world's poorest countries, housing and diet are of poor quality. Along with limited access to health care, these factors lead to high infant mortality rates and short life expectancy.

Lesson Vocabulary

literacy rate   the proportion of a nation's population over age 15 that can read and write

life expectancy   the average expected life span of an individual

infant mortality rate   the number of deaths that occur in the first year of life per 1,000 live births

TOPIC 10 LESSON 5

Lesson Summary
GROWTH, RESOURCES, AND DEVELOPMENT

MODIFIED CORNELL NOTES

Rapid population growth is a serious problem in many less developed countries. The **population growth rate**, the increase of a country's population in a year, including births, deaths, and migrations, averages about 1.8 percent in LDCs. Many LDCs are experiencing an increase in life expectancy, and birth rates far outpace deaths. This leads to rapid population growth. Increased populations require increased job opportunities, health and education facilities, industrial and agricultural production, and exports and imports.

The uneven distribution of natural resources throughout the world also affects development. Some nations lack mineral resources or fertile farmland.

LDCs often lack the physical and human capital necessary to develop resources. Without physical capital, industry cannot grow and agricultural output will remain low. Human capital, the skills and knowledge of workers, is critical to economic development. Access to education is limited in LDCs, and literacy rates are low, especially for girls, who often have fewer opportunities than boys. When a country does not have sufficient human capital, it lacks the skilled workers necessary to manage industries.

Other problems for LDCs are health and political issues. Many people in LDCs suffer from **malnutrition**, or inadequate nutrition. Political factors have limited the development of many poor nations. These include a history of colonialism or central planning, civil war, and corrupt or unstable governments.

A country can use two methods to finance its economic development. **Internal financing** comes from citizens' savings. In less developed countries, however, citizens have little money to save. For that reason, most LDCs finance development with **foreign investment**, external investment originating from other countries. There are two types of foreign investment. **Foreign direct investment (FDI)** is the establishment of an enterprise by a

(Continues on the next page.)

Lesson Vocabulary

population growth rate   a measure of how rapidly a country's population increases in a given year

malnutrition   consistently inadequate nutrition

internal financing   capital derived from the savings of a country's own citizens

foreign investment   capital that originates in other countries, either by foreign direct investment or foreign portfolio investment

foreign direct investment   this occurs when investors establish a business in another country

MODIFIED CORNELL NOTES

foreigner. Much foreign direct investment comes from multinational corporations, large corporations that produce and sell throughout the world. **Foreign portfolio investment** occurs when foreigners invest in a country's stock and bond markets, often by purchasing shares in mutual funds.

Foreign governments may give money to LDCs for development or disaster relief. Foreign aid can be motivated by humanitarian concerns. At the same time, developed nations have military, political, economic, and cultural reasons to extend aid to LDCs.

International economic institutions also promote development. The World Bank, the largest provider of development assistance, offers loans, advice, and other resources to LDCs. The United Nations Development Program (UNDP) is dedicated to the elimination of poverty through development. The International Monetary Fund (IMF), originally created to stabilize international exchange rates, has expanded its role to promote development. The IMF offers advice and technical assistance to LDCs. It can also help LDCs that are having trouble repaying a debt to a nation that lent it money. It does this by helping to arrange **debt rescheduling**, lengthening the time of repayment and forgiving or dismissing part of the loan. In return, the LDC agrees to accept a **stabilization program**, changing its economic policies to meet IMF goals.

Some private aid groups also work to help LDCs build their economies. **Nongovernmental organizations (NGOs)** are independent groups that raise money to fund aid and development programs. Examples include the Red Cross, CARE, and the World Wildlife Fund.

Lesson Vocabulary

foreign portfolio investment   foreign investors making purchases in another country's financial markets

debt rescheduling   an agreement between a lending nation and a debtor nation whereby the lending nation lengthens the time of debt repayment and forgives, or dismisses, part of the loan and, in return, the LDC agrees to accept a stabilization program

stabilization program   the changing of a nation's economic policies to meet IMF goals

nongovernmental organizations   independent groups that raise money to fund aid and development programs

TOPIC 10 LESSON 6 — Lesson Summary
CHANGING ECONOMIES

Many LDCs are making the difficult transition from centrally planned economies to free markets. One step in this transition is **privatization,** the sale or transfer of state-owned businesses to individuals. Another step is to change the legal system to guarantee and protect private property rights. Inefficient businesses may fail in a competitive system, leading to rising unemployment and unrest.

Russia is an example of a country that completely threw out its centrally planned economy and replaced it with one based on free markets. Until the late 1980s, Russia was part of the communist Soviet Union. But communism and the Soviet Union itself collapsed in 1991. Russians experienced hardships as they moved quickly to a market-based economy. Without price controls, prices of many goods soared. Billions of dollars flooded the country from the IMF and other institutions, but because of mismanagement and corruption, the funds were not used efficiently. By 1998, the Russian economy was in a shambles. Tight controls from the central government, combined with rising prices for Russian oil, allowed Russian leaders to stem the crisis and repay foreign debt.

China is a communist country that modified its centrally planned economy with some free market practices. Farmers and factory managers were given more freedom to make decisions about what to produce and how much to charge for it. China set up hundreds of **special economic zones,** designated regions where foreign investment is encouraged. Since the start of these reforms, China's economy has grown tremendously. China is the world's largest exporter of goods and a key trading partner of the United States. Still, economic development has not meant political liberty.

In the 1990s, India's government began to invite foreign investment and promote other free market practices. One area of significant growth was in high-technology industries. Economic growth helped promote the emergence of a much larger middle class. Urban dwellers with education and skills benefit the most from growth. Uneducated people in poor rural areas struggle with poverty and continue to rely on subsistence farming.

(Continues on the next page.)

Lesson Vocabulary

privatization   the sale or transfer of government-owned businesses to individuals

special economic zones   designated regions that operate under different economic laws from the rest of the country in order to attract foreign investment and promote exports

TOPIC 10 LESSON 6
Lesson Summary
CHANGING ECONOMIES (continued)

Some North African nations have built productive economies. This success is mainly due to large reserves of oil. Only two African nations south of the Sahara have sizable economies—South Africa and Nigeria.

In Latin America, the two biggest success stories are Brazil and Mexico. Both countries have abundant resources. Both have taken steps to make their economies more diverse. Brazil has become a strong manufacturing power, producing everything from vehicles to shoes. Like Brazil, Mexico has diversified its economy by promoting its tourism industry and building factories. By diversifying their economies, Mexico and Brazil have freed 80 percent or more of their labor forces from farm work.

TOPIC 10 Lesson Summary
LESSON 7   GLOBALIZATION

The increasingly tight interconnection of producers, consumers, and financial systems around the world is known as **globalization**. Several factors contribute to the ever-tightening links between economies around the world. They include the development of faster methods of communication and transportation, the widespread adoption of elements of the free enterprise system, and the growth of international trade agreements.

Today's communications revolution connect customers and suppliers on opposite sides of the world. The opening of more free market economies has created new investment opportunities. Regional trading blocs tie nations together in an interconnected world economy.

Globalization also poses challenges. A financial crisis in one country affects other countries because the world financial markets are closely connected. Multinational corporations are a fact of globalization, but critics claim that multinationals do little to aid less developed countries because most of the profits go to foreign owners. Much of the debate over multinationals and globalization focuses on the impact on less developed countries. However, people in developed nations are equally concerned about a related issue—the loss of jobs as companies move part of their operations to overseas.

Globalization and development have accelerated population shifts. In many less developed countries, cities offer more job opportunities than rural areas. As a result, large numbers of people in villages are streaming into cities. Each year, millions of workers leave less developed countries in the hopes of finding jobs in developed nations. Once they find work, many immigrants send regular cash payments to their families back home. These **remittances** provide an important source of income. At the same time, many well-trained and educated people also leave LDCs for well-paying jobs in developed nations. This **"brain drain"** may hurt development by siphoning off vital human capital.

(Continues on the next page.)

Lesson Vocabulary

globalization   the increasingly tight interconnection of producers, consumers, and financial systems around the world

remittances   cash payments sent by workers who have migrated to a new country to family members in their home country

brain drain   the migration of the best-educated people of less developed countries to developed nations

Name _____ Class _____ Date _____

MODIFIED CORNELL NOTES

Globalization has created new opportunities but also new challenges for the world's economies. Some of these challenges have become sources of tension between the developed world and the developing world. Issues related to equal treatment and the environment are key causes of conflict, as is competition for scarce resources.

Environmental scientists—mostly based in developed nations—worry that rapid development can cause environmental damage. They seek to promote **sustainable development**, that is, the goal of meeting current development needs without using up the resources needed by future generations. One major issue that crosses national borders and impacts the world is **deforestation**, or large-scale destruction of forests.

Globalization poses challenges even for the world's most successful economy—our own. For the United States to compete in global markets, American workers must be ready to respond to changes in the workplace. And American companies must continue their long tradition of innovation.

Lesson Vocabulary

sustainable development   the goal of meeting current development needs without using up resources needed by future generations

deforestation   the large-scale destruction of forests

Name _____ Class _____ Date _____

Answer the questions below using the information in the Lesson Summaries on the previous pages.

Lesson 1: Why Nations Trade

1. What is absolute advantage, and how is it related to resource use?

_____

_____

2. Synthesize Why does the law of comparative advantage make sense based on resource use?

_____

_____

Lesson 2: Trade Barriers and Agreements

3. How are import quotas and tariffs similar?

_____

_____

4. Draw Inferences How do tariffs on U.S. goods benefit U.S. consumers?

_____

_____

Lesson 3: Exchange Rates and Trade

5. How is the fixed exchange-rate system different from the flexible exchange-rate system?

_____

_____

6. Draw Inferences Suppose you traveled to Mexico before exchange rates had been established. What would the impact of this be?

_____

_____

Lesson 4: Development

7. Identify some aspects of the average American's life that reflect the high level of development of the United States.

_____

_____

8. Draw Conclusions How do the economic advances made by developed countries help the newly industrialized countries (NICs) make progress more quickly?

_____

_____

Name _____ Class _____ Date _____

Lesson 5: Growth, Resources, and Development

9. What is meant by the term *human capital*? Why is human capital necessary to move beyond mere subsistence?

_____

_____

10. **Draw Inferences** What do you think the United States' population growth rate of 0.7 percent might mean for you in the future? How could it affect the economies of the United States and other developed countries?

_____

_____

Lesson 6: Changing Economies

11. What steps can a government take to privatize businesses?

_____

_____

12. **Identify Supporting Details** Why do there need to be changes in the legal system when transitioning to a market economy?

_____

_____

Lesson 7: Globalization

13. What factors have led to globalization?

_____

_____

14. **Assess an Argument** In the Middle Ages, merchants traveling along the Silk Road carried not only goods but also ideas. This aspect of globalization is still happening today. Do you agree? Explain.

_____

_____